# UNLOCKING DIVERSITY

SECOND EDITION
EXPANDED AND UPDATED

FOR THE MODERN-DAY LEADER

# UNLOCKING DIVERSITY

## Your Guide to Becoming an Inclusive Leader Beyond Surface Level

**SECONDE NIMENYA, MBA**

Author of *A Long Way to School*

Copyright ©2025 by Seconde Nimenya

All Rights Reserved. No part of this book may be reproduced or used in whole or in part, transmitted in any form or by any means: electronic, mechanical, or other, now known or hereafter invented, including xerography, photocopying, and recording, without written permission from the author/publisher, except for "fair use" as brief quotations in a review.

This is a nonfiction work. All facts, conversations, people, historical events, and places mentioned in this book have been reconstructed to the best of the author's recollection. Some of the names and characteristics of individuals mentioned in this book have been changed or omitted to protect their identities.

Second Edition
Published in the United States
ISBN 979-8-9936926-5-4 (Paperback)
ISBN 979-8-9936926-8-5 (eBook)

Library of Congress Control Number: 2020909222
Names: Nimenya, Seconde, author.
Title: Unlocking Diversity: Your Guide to Becoming an Inclusive Leader Beyond Surface Level / Seconde Nimenya.

Subjects: Diversity, equity, and inclusion (DEI), belonging, leadership, inclusive workplace culture, business management, business and leadership, organizational effectiveness, inclusive leader, organizational learning, leadership education, leadership coaching, leadership training, leadership consulting, multicultural marketing, employee development, employee motivation, employee engagement, cultural diversity, work-life balance, stay at home parents, women and gender gap, gender equality, feminism, generation gap, global development, women empowerment, African studies, cross cultural communication, race conversations, race in America, immigration, black experience, migrations, psychological safety, cultural competency, selling in multicultural markets, customer management, racial discrimination, privilege, social identity, cultural sensitivity, cultural fluency, unconscious bias, immigrants, emotional intelligence, empathy, equality, inequality, human resources management, personnel management, DEI practitioners, DEI advocates, books on DEI, business coaching, thought leadership.

# CONTENTS

| | |
|---|---|
| PREFACE | vii |
| INTRODUCTION: FIRST WORLD PROBLEMS | 1 |
| CHAPTER 1: UNLOCKING CULTURAL EXPECTATIONS | 13 |
| CHAPTER 2: THE CONTRASTS OF LIFE | 21 |
| CHAPTER 3: RACE IN AMERICA: THE ELEPHANT IN THE ROOM | 25 |
| CHAPTER 4: THE BLACK EXPERIENCE | 37 |
| CHAPTER 5: WORKING WITH GRANDPA: WORKPLACE AND THE GENERATION GAP | 45 |
| CHAPTER 6: WOMEN AND WORK-LIFE (UN)BALANCE | 55 |
| CHAPTER 7: SHOULD STAY-AT-HOME MOTHERS GET SOCIAL SECURITY? | 63 |
| CHAPTER 8: RECOGNIZING PRIVILEGE | 69 |
| CHAPTER 9: EMBRACING CULTURAL INTEGRATION | 87 |
| CHAPTER 10: FINDING COMMON PURPOSE | 95 |
| CHAPTER 11: DOING BUSINESS IN A MULTICULTURAL MARKET | 101 |
| CHAPTER 12: BELONGING AND WORKPLACE CULTURE | 125 |
| CHAPTER 13: WORKING AS A DEI PRACTITIONER | 133 |
| CHAPTER 14: CREATING A RIPPLE OF INCLUSIVE CULTURES | 153 |
| SUMMING IT UP | 165 |
| GLOSSARY OF INCLUSIVE LEADERSHIP TERMS | 173 |
| NOTES | 181 |
| ABOUT THE AUTHOR | 183 |
| BECHANGE GROUP COACHING AND TRAINING | 185 |
| INVITE SECONDE NIMENYA TO SPEAK AT YOUR NEXT EVENT | 186 |
| ALSO, BY SECONDE NIMENYA | 187 |

# PREFACE

## Is there a different way to enhance equity, equality, and inclusion?

As I prepared this second edition in early 2025, media reports indicated that the current White House administration was in the process of terminating all Diversity, Equity, and Inclusion (DEI)- related mandates, policies, programs, preferences, and activities across the federal government. This executive order represented a significant shift from the previous administration's approach, which had implemented various DEI initiatives to advance equity and inclusion.

Curious to see how organizations were responding to the executive order, I came across this article published in the Detroit News. The headline read: *"McKinsey champions diversity while rivals abandon targets."* [1]

Despite the executive order for firms to eliminate DEI policies, McKinsey & Co. decided to keep committing to workforce diversity. The article went on to mention some of the major companies that have decided to abandon or reduce their DEI initiatives.

In this second edition, I wanted to share some food for thought on the myths, misunderstandings, and even mishaps of DEI, and why we still need it to advance equity and inclusion in our society. The first edition of this book came out in 2020, during the COVID-19 pandemic, and it was a time of upheaval that unmasked some of the social justice issues that had been swept under the rug.

One of the uprisings happened as a reaction to the global protests triggered by the death of George Floyd, a Black man who was killed by a police officer in Minneapolis, Minnesota, on May 25, 2020. This incident led to a significant social movement, with demonstrations spreading far beyond the United States.

This updated and expanded edition includes new stories and fresh insights that were not covered in the first edition.

Chapters 1 and 2 set the tone for exploring cultural differences from both the individual and collective mindsets. Chapters 3 and 4 explain the theme of diversity, equity, and inclusion from the perspective of race in America and the black experience.

The second edition introduces new content, including Chapters 5, 6, and 7, and delves into the complexities of diversity, equity, and inclusion in the workplace, particularly focusing on multigenerational dynamics as discussed in Chapter 5: "Working with Grandpa: The Generation Gap."

Chapters 6 and 7 address the myths and realities of work-life balance for mothers. These chapters present insights from research by Beike Biotechnology on whether stay-at-home parents should receive social security and other benefits to compensate for their opportunity costs.

Chapter 8 unpacks the concept of *privilege,* as it is a term sometimes misunderstood relating to diversity, equity, and inclusion. Chapter 9 is about cultural integration as opposed to cultural assimilation. Chapter 10 discusses finding common ground and bridging gaps between systems, institutions, and people. Chapter 11 presents a case on how to do business in a multicultural market.

Also new is chapter 12, which examines the concept of workplace culture and belonging and tackles the dilemma employees often face about how much personal information to share at work, specifically what constitutes too much information — or *TMI*.

Chapter 13 examines the best practices, pitfalls, challenges, and opportunities of working as a DEI practitioner. The final chapter, 14, "Creating a Ripple of Inclusive Cultures," summarizes the key points and provides a roadmap for embarking on the journey to become an inclusive leader beyond surface level, both personally and professionally.

So, read on.

# INTRODUCTION

## First World Problems

A few years ago, a friend sent me a video titled *First World Problems*.[2] After I watched it, I had mixed feelings. On the one hand, I acknowledged how people perceive problems as real, as opposed to *non-real* ones. One such example was an African kid in the video, reading one of the First World problems as: "I hate it when my phone charger won't reach my bed." Now, I do hate it when my iPhone charger doesn't reach my bed, even though my previous Samsung did. But, instead of complaining about it, I got creative. At night, when I charge my phone, I just put it on a box on the floor beside my bed and plug it into the power outlet. Miraculously, it reaches my nightstand!

I know what real problems mean, and my phone not reaching my nightstand is not one of them. I also know that, in one way or another, we all encounter problems that can be perceived as small, medium, or big. The best way to understand this difference in our perception can be found in Abraham Maslow's Hierarchy of Needs.[3]

From Maslow's hierarchy or pyramid of needs, we learn that humans have three major categories of needs:

1. **Basic Needs**—This category includes our physiological needs, such as food, water, warmth, rest (including sleep), and safety.

2. **Psychological Needs**—This category includes belonging and love needs, such as intimate relationships and friendships, and esteem needs, like having prestige and feelings of accomplishment.
3. **Self-Fulfillment Needs**—This category includes what Maslow called "self-actualization," in which one achieves one's full potential, including creative endeavors.

I must confess, when I learned this theory at the university in a psychology class, I didn't really grasp what I was learning. I thought our professor was just harassing my brain, making me memorize useless information. Now, as a teacher and student of life myself, I find Maslow's theory very useful and important.

So, when I watched that video on First World problems, I asked myself, "What exactly are First World problems? And are there any Second World problems? And what qualifies as Third World problems?"

That is how I started writing on power, privilege, and purpose in Chapter 8: Recognizing Privilege. I had planned for it to be this book's first chapter, but then I realized I had more to say on topics that all relate to "privilege," a word somehow despised by some, and accepted by others, depending on your perspective.

The *First World Problems* video makes an important point on what types of problems we should or shouldn't complain about. I have had the privilege of living in three different countries—my native Burundi, in Africa, Canada, and the United States—and in different socio-economic environments, so I understand what those in the video were implying when it comes to Third World problems as opposed to First World problems. It all comes down to our human needs and where we stand on the pyramid in having those needs met.

Depending on our life circumstances, we have different needs at different times in our lives. While it may be safe to say Third World problems are those experienced by people who live in Third World nations, also known as *developing nations*, there is a nuance. What people sometimes fail to acknowledge is that not everyone in the developing world experiences the same problems and in the same way. This thinking also applies to those living in the First World, namely, developed countries. Not everyone in developed countries is on the same level when it comes to having their human needs met.

The way we perceive our problems has to do with whether or not we acknowledge our privilege. Once we have met our basic needs, it is okay to aspire to get our psychological and self-fulfillment needs met. It is a natural part of the human experience to aspire for more in life. The higher we climb on the pyramid of needs, the more privilege we have, and the more we can do to uplift those who still struggle to get their basic needs met. I hope that is the lesson the director of *First World Problems* wanted us to learn. Those who commented saying that people in the First World have real problems too are not wrong.

First World problems are not just frivolous concerns like whether our iPhone charger reaches our nightstand, but real problems like health issues, wealth disparities, and homelessness.

However, although not a guarantee, it is much more likely that our basic needs will be met if we live in a First World country. And once our basic needs are met, we can aspire to overcome First World challenges.

Appreciating what we already have might be the first step in overcoming such problems. I used to tell my children that wanting gluten-free food, when so many kids around the world, even in some of the richest countries, were hungry, was definitely a First World problem. However, my kids have explained to me that gluten intolerance is a real health issue. So, I have learned not to diminish the suffering of people with celiac disease; they have a real problem that affects their health, and we should all be compassionate enough to understand that just because we do not have the problem, it doesn't mean others do not suffer from it.

This type of misconception can often increase stereotypes and even create biases, which I will share throughout this book, and specifically in Chapter 4: *The Black Experience*.

With this book, my aim is to take you on a journey of reflection. I invite you to consider our current social environment and explore how we can find a common purpose, live together in harmony and respect, and enrich one another's diverse experiences. It is in our diversity of experiences that we can find innovation, creativity, and business opportunities. I hope you will take this journey with me to discover not only how different we are, but also how common our purposes can be. Let us embark on this adventure we call life with an open mind and a loving heart.

This book is a collection of my reflections shared in an attempt to bridge the gaps in our diverse and multicultural communities, connect people with a common purpose, and do my part for our collective healing. They are mostly from my observations when I interact with people in my work as a speaker on the topics of inclusive leadership, as well as personal growth. I have had the pleasure of meeting people from diverse backgrounds, and as an observer, I take my time to notice how people behave in various situations.

When you encounter people who act differently from you, instead of making assumptions about why they act the way they do, ask yourself: *What is it about me they find different, and what is it about them I find different?* After you have identified the differences in yourself and others, decide how you want to respond. Do you want to make the gap in your differences even wider? Or do you want to reduce it and eventually bridge it? Our differences can be the catalyst for a good conversation, and even a good business connection. Some people see strangers when they meet someone they don't know; others seize the opportunity to make new friends and acquaintances. That is why I love to travel. It allows me to meet new people and see how different we are, and yet, at our very core, I realize we are not all that different. We have all stereotyped those we perceive as different.

Stereotypes are blinders that prevent us from seeing the situation for what it is; people tend to jump to conclusions based on their individual or collective histories. Often, we use stereotyping to build a protective shield. And all this comes from our experiences, which affect our behaviors. It doesn't matter who we are; we all have biases. My work in the field of diversity and inclusion has allowed me to take a step back and not assume the worst immediately when it comes to people's reactions to differences. But that is not to say, "I've got this," when it comes to understanding diversity. I am still flawed like everyone else, and I have my biases. I also try to learn and grow from my limitations.

When someone tells you how they feel about being stereotyped, instead of being defensive or worse, quick to dismiss the issue, please stop and listen. Then ask questions and get clarification.

People cannot read minds, but they can feel your energy through your emotions and verbal and nonverbal communication.

I have been working in the diversity and inclusion field for more than fifteen years now, and I still find it both fascinating and intimidating. Fascinating because I get to share my life lessons with other people, and I learn from different situations. But it is also intimidating because I recognize the difficulty in changing human behaviors, especially when those behaviors are deeply rooted in conditioning based on past experiences, or when we cannot relate to those who suffer from social and economic inequities. Writing or talking about the theme of diversity and inclusion is hard because you cannot share personal perspectives without running the risk of alienating some individuals. People are wired differently, and I constantly have to remind myself of this basic fact. No one book is going to satisfy everyone. That is why my intention is not to change people's behaviors, but to offer insights to help expand mindsets on how we can all benefit from the power of our diversity, because every one of us has a diversity story. While we are different, we also crave a sense of belonging, feeling connected, and being accepted for who we are. That is why it is in everyone's interest to create inclusive cultures, whether it's in our workplaces or in our diverse communities.

One question I repeatedly ask myself is: *If diversity and inclusion are good for us and our businesses, why do we still have a hard time creating inclusive cultures?*

I know for sure we all have unconscious bias at some level. What matters is what we do to overcome our bias, including exploring our humanity and extending kindness and understanding to those who experience discrimination because of who they are. This book is my way of answering the above question by showing you how you can live, learn, and lead in a world of differences. While reading this book might not help you end bias and prejudice today, it will help spark your inquisitive mind so you can help me answer the above question. It will also help you increase your awareness and learn new habits, while unlearning old beliefs that no longer have a place in our society.

By acknowledging our own biases and working to overcome them ourselves, we can help disrupt discrimination and other social injustices and help create inclusive cultures where everyone can thrive. My goal for this book is to share reflections that support individuals and professionals with balanced perspectives on how to incorporate diversity and inclusion, not just as something nice to have in your organization, or to merely invest in, but as a core driver for business success.

My hope is that you can use the perspectives I share to support you in your mission and your day-to-day leadership. Choosing to be a leader is a privilege afforded to all of us, beginning with our personal leadership, but only a few make that choice. I realize being a leader is not a simple task because personal leadership involves only you. Leadership is what you do when no one is watching you or appraising your work. It is what you do when the lights go down and you take off your social mask. It is how you behave when the fans go home, and you face yourself in the privacy of your mind.

Whatever you do in your leadership moments becomes the fine definition of your integrity. My definition of integrity is: What you do when things don't necessarily go your way, or when no one is praising you or your work. That is when your true personal leadership is tested, and your true colors come out. What you choose to do in those moments will be a testimony to your courage, resilience, passion, and purpose, all features of good leadership. And I believe that is the kind of leadership we need to model and teach to our younger generations.

Personal integrity is a much-needed ingredient if you want to be a great leader, not just personally, but also professionally. I was talking with a friend one day when I used the term integrity in relation to work. My friend joked, "But, Seconde, integrity is not gonna pay my mortgage!" You know what? My friend was right. Integrity is not going to pay your mortgage because integrity is intangible. It is also an often-unappreciated quality in our socio-political environment. But I would still choose integrity over hype because, when all else fails, integrity is something you can fall back on, knowing you did the best you could with what you had or knew at that moment. Yes, indeed, integrity might not pay your mortgage, or even get you a date, but you need it to live as sanely as possible in a seemingly insane world.

As you browse through the reflections in this book, I hope they will allow you to see yourself in a new light, overcome your leadership limitations, and expand your awareness in every area of your life. Then you will be empowered to move from being an unconscious leader to an advocate for inclusive cultures in a world of differences. And to get you started on this journey, below I will share the stages involved in awakening our mindsets.

In my diversity, equity, and inclusion work, I have observed that people's behaviors toward diversity mainly show up in three mindset stages: unconscious, evolving, and conscious. In each stage, people behave in a certain way. Let us look at the behaviors associated with each of these mindset stages.

## The Unconscious Mindset

When you operate in this mindset, you don't take time to think about what other people may be going through. And when it comes to implicit bias, you almost operate on autopilot, exhibiting behaviors without much reflection on what it might do to those who are marginalized or not represented. Unconscious bias results from our brains reacting to the differences in people. It often leads to responses dictated by fear. Considerable research confirms that every person has biases, whether they are aware of it or not.

Some bias is conscious, of course, but in this section, our emphasis is on unconscious bias operating from an unconscious mindset. Therefore, biases can dictate how you perceive others compared to yourself, and how you make decisions, including decisions about whom you want to do business with, employ, or marry. With an unconscious mindset, your mind is blurred by bias blind spots that can have a lasting effect on your perception of others and potentially influence how you treat those different from you.

Many people choose to interact with people who look like them because, implicitly, they feel more at ease. The problem with this perception is that at the unconscious level, you may or may not favor someone solely based on their social or cultural background, because they fit some group stereotype of those likely to succeed, or those pre-determined to be rich or famous—whatever the perception might be.

## The Evolving Mindset

The second stage of the awareness awakening is the evolving mindset. People with an evolving mindset constantly check to see where they are on their awareness journey. They are aware of what is around them. Even though they might operate with an unconscious mindset at times, they are willing to stop, reflect, and correct their course. They are willing to work on themselves to be more aware and to overcome bias, whether perpetrated against them or by them. They are cognizant of the disadvantages of living in an unconscious mindset, and they constantly try to keep evolving. When they make mistakes, they are more willing to admit to them and learn from them. This level of awareness results from trial and error, and I think many, if not most of us, operate at this level of awareness. Make no mistake; it is not a bad stage to be at! But at the same time, don't stay there. Keep working on your consciousness; release your unconscious mindset until you reach the final stage: the conscious mindset.

## The Conscious Mindset

At this level, people are aware of their power to make changes in themselves and others. They carefully choose their actions with intention, acknowledge the differences in themselves and others, and are not threatened by diverse people and ideas. They know their worth, respect themselves, and extend that same respect to others.

People with a conscious mindset choose to respond rather than react, and they learn what they don't know instead of assuming. They tend to meet people where they are on their evolving journey and help them grow. They value other people's stories, experiences, and input. They do not alienate those who might disagree with their thinking; they invite the differing voices into a dialogue because they know multiple perspectives are always needed to solve problems. People who operate from a conscious mindset strive to share balanced points of view.

When you reach this state of awareness, you become a strong advocate for diversity, inclusion, and equity because you are no longer threatened by differences in yourself and others. You know it is no longer just about your journey; it is about who else you can bring with you on the journey. You start leading from the heart because you have established your humanity and see others' humanity. You empathize and create spaces of belonging and inclusiveness wherever you have the most power to do so. At this stage, you unleash your gifts to serve your fellow humans and not just those who look, pray, and speak like you, have the same gender or sexual identity as you, live in the same community as you, or adhere to your social class and political affiliation.

When we unlock diversity, inclusion happens, and when there's inclusion, equity follows. This whole book is about expanding our consciousness and increasing understanding of one another, not through debates, but through reflection and conversations. It is about peeling back the layers of our human complexities to return to our most authentic selves.

In these pages, I invite you to come with me on a journey to unlock our human potential and to build a world where everyone is accepted for who they are and what they bring to make it a better place for all.

# CHAPTER 1

## Unlocking Cultural Expectations

Changing times require changing and evolving mindsets. And every generation has had to decide what kind of legacy to leave to the next. What is happening in our world today allows us to decide on the legacy we want for our children and our grandchildren. It is also an opportunity to show that the real world is made of opposites. As John Steinbeck said, "What good is the warmth of summer, without the cold of winter to give it sweetness."

Life is a constant balancing act of joy and sorrow, good and evil, bad politics and good politics; and sometimes, evil and good cohabitating right in ourselves, in our families, in our communities, and in our leaders. Moreover, we cannot enjoy life if there is no death, recognize light if there is no darkness, or enjoy peace if we have never experienced conflict. Humans live in constant opposites, whether on the physical, mental, or spiritual level.

We also find these opposing worlds in our socio-economic systems. Sometimes, people blame economic and social systems, whether it be capitalism or socialism, a collectivist or an individualistic society, for what is not working in our world. But I believe no perfect economic or social model exists. People who live in collectivist societies cannot expect people from individualistic societies to understand them right away, and vice versa.

That is why we often experience friction between the "we" and the "I", or "them" versus "us" mentality. However, that doesn't mean both models cannot cohabitate harmoniously, with understanding, give and take, teaching and learning from each other's strengths and limitations. Let's take a few moments to reflect on each of these societal models.

## Collectivist Societies

Part of what makes collectivist societies strong is the connection between individuals and communities and the way they help each other in times of need. The downside of this model is that it can also mean a lack of individual liberty for self-expression. This lack can stifle possibilities as to how one goes about fulfilling their life purpose. Also, collectivist societies dictate what's good for all, without regard for how it may affect individuals. Another downside is that if you stay within the bounds of your cultural comfort zone, you don't stretch to connect with those who have different cultural customs.

I grew up in the collectivist model, and it continues to affect my decision-making. Even when publishing my first book, *Evolving Through Adversity*, a true account of my life, I was inhibited, reluctant to share so many personal details with the world, especially concerning my family dynamics. A constant, nagging voice told me I was sharing way too much. "Oh, no, you didn't! Why would you want to put yourself out there, Seconde? That's not how your collective society does it."

But I decided, at least for me, it was important to explore and heal my wounds because I knew if I waited for my community to give me permission, I would never get it.

The other thing about collectivist societies is that they often lack a sense of personal accountability when dealing with issues that affect individuals, such as domestic violence or sexual harassment. For example, when I was a little girl in elementary school, some boys bullied my friends and me every single day after school. We couldn't report them to our parents or the school authorities because we were girls and they were boys. Our parents and the school authorities would have assumed we were fooling around with them. In my culture, girls were always the ones in trouble because we were told to avoid boys and, especially, not to "provoke" them. As a girl, whenever you reported being harassed by a man or boy, your parents said something like, "What were you doing with him? It's your own fault. Why were you with him in the first place?" Our parents rarely took a girl's side or questioned the boy's or man's motives. According to my culture, it was the girl's fault if a boy harassed her. If my friends and I had reported it, no one would have taken our side or defended us. And so, my two best friends and I stayed silent and endured harassment for many months.

Finally, I could no longer take the harassment, so I told my friends, "Hey, girls, we need to stand up for ourselves and stop the bullies from harassing us." My friends thought I was crazy since I was the tiniest of us three. But I insisted we had to do something if we wanted to stay in school and live. The next day, the bullies started following us. As soon as we saw them, my friends started running. So much for standing up for ourselves. But I refused to run. I stood there and faced the bullies. When one of the boys started touching my hand, I pushed him. Then I said, "I am going to report you to my parents, who will tell my school, and the school will tell your parents. You guys are going to get in big trouble!"

How I thought about saying that I don't know. It was an empty threat, of course, because I wasn't planning on telling my parents, and it would have been a waste of time anyway. After a couple of minutes of confrontation, the boys gave up and ran, calling me names as they left, which didn't bother me.

My friends had been watching the whole confrontation from their hiding place. They looked like frightened little chickens and were amazed I had not been killed. They couldn't believe that tiny me had saved them from the bullies. That day, we ran home, happy and free. We never saw the bullies again. We later learned they were school dropouts who certainly had too much time on their hands. They were also teenagers with brains rushing with hormones. Our parents and the school authorities never found out about our boy trouble because we dealt with it.

Today, at least in the United States, we are seeing a shift in the culture of sexual harassment and what it means to consent or not. I am not sure other cultures and subcultures know how to deal with this shift yet. Things like the *Time's Up* or the *Me Too* movements happening in the Western world can be confusing for many collectivist societies. The main reason is that, for a long time, women in those cultures learned to *deal with it,* according to their cultural norms, for the sake of their collective well-being. Women were not supposed to voice their opinions or objections, especially against men in their communities.

I know it is still a gray area in my culture of origin. I met a woman who told me about an incident where she was sexually harassed in an office setting. I asked, "Why didn't you tell your husband?" She replied, "Because if I did, he would say I was seducing the man, so it would still be my fault." In many cases, staying silent is how women have had to deal with sexual harassment because they fear upsetting their husbands, fathers, and all the other male authority figures in their communities.

Among first-generation female Americans—the daughters of immigrants—the confusion is even greater. The upside for most immigrants who come from collectivist societies and form their communities in the United States is that they have a sense of shared culture and togetherness. It is easier to retain one's cultural habits and feel connected to those with similar origins. Even the immigrants' children come to rely on this sense of community to learn about their parents' origins and feel connected to their motherland. Immigrant parents like myself have taught our children to consider the females of their mothers' generation as their *aunties*, and the men as their *uncles*, and to respect and trust them as such.

However, what we didn't teach our younger generation was how to discern when *uncle* was starting to act weird and making sexual innuendos, and what to do in that instance. Should they tell their parents? Yes, they can come to us and tell us about the situation. But that may not fix the problem because parents might be afraid of confronting the transgressor for the sake of the community. I have heard some men complain about the *Me Too* movement, saying things like: "The Me Too movement is a women's exaggeration and unnecessary." I couldn't even articulate how disconcerted I was by that remark. I guess that is why I am writing about it.

When people question why women do not report sexual harassment cases or report them when it is too late to be believed, it is partly because in many cultures, society does not take the woman's side. In most cases, women end up being ostracized by their community, so they prefer to stay silent. And to be honest, that is how women in general have dealt with abuse, sexual harassment, and domestic violence for generations. Even in non-collectivist societies, women still face these challenges, despite standing up for themselves. This is a deep societal issue that needs the attention of not only women, but men as well, and from diverse cultures.

What can we do to lessen cultural hindrances in collectivist societies? My experiences from living in different parts of the world have allowed me to come to this realization: All of us from diverse communities can still honor our cultures of origin while learning to let go of cultural practices that don't honor who we are. This chapter is my sort of wink to multicultural communities, and here is what I want to share: Before we expect someone else to fix the issues in our communities, we should first look inward and fix the issues ourselves. Issues related to generational gaps, sexual harassment, and domestic violence are problems we can work on and solve both individually and collectively. In addition, we need to reach out to other community stakeholders, form alliances to share what works and doesn't work, learn from our mistakes, and practice some course-correcting.

## Individualistic Societies

The opposite of a collectivist society is an individualistic society. One of the upsides of this social system is that the individual controls their destiny. It gives people leeway to share their gifts in a freer environment without having to consult the group.

The downside of this model is that the individual is only valued by society for certain accomplishments they can show outwardly. There is also a lack of connections when you need them most. Although this reality is on a per-case basis, there is a higher risk for individualistic communities to have high levels of mental health and other negative signs of social isolation.

## The Harmony of Opposites

Of course, while we would like to pick one perfect societal model to stick to, there is no perfect model or system. Society must determine what works and doesn't work. Practicing the wisdom of the harmony of opposites by mixing the two societal systems could improve social connections and quality of life. You would have a community-based society, and at the same time, space for individual growth to explore your full potential. You would have the opportunity to help yourself but also be able to support others without losing your identity in the collective. In addition, you would have the freedom to speak against whatever doesn't work in your community, share your opinions without fear of being ostracized, and have the backing of your community.

Therefore, the collective and individualistic models are not mutually exclusive. And for the dual model to be successful, both the personal and collective would have to find balance, including a political component of legislation that would foster personal creativity and critical thinking, while bridging the two systems with social incentives to bring people together more harmoniously, giving and taking from diverse communities to enrich cultural diversity. In this way, the cultural mix can occur naturally, without imposing one system over another. Everyone in society would benefit from sharing cultural practices that promote inclusion, innovation, and connections in a welcoming environment.

We can learn so much about the harmony of opposites from nature. In nature, all forces are beneficial; both positive and negative forces are needed and coexist and balance each other. For us humans, we have the bonus of being able to think. Therefore, if we want to live in harmony, we need to first acknowledge our opposing sides, realize that we carry both the light and shadow in our psyche, so we can turn the negative force into a positive one, and never take more than we are willing to give, because it creates an imbalance.

# CHAPTER 2

## The Contrasts of Life

*"There is no light without shadow
and no psychic wholeness without imperfection."*
— Carl G. Jung

Like Abraham Maslow, Carl Jung, the Swiss psychiatrist and psychoanalyst, is another great thinker whose theories I studied in my undergraduate human psychology class. At that time, I focused more on memorizing the theories and ensuring I passed my class, rather than understanding their real-life applications. It wasn't until later when I began observing the human behavior— including my own— that I truly grasped its importance.

Jung's "light" and "shadow" metaphor illustrates the dualities of the human mind, emphasizing both our conscious awareness and unconscious selves. We must embrace both our light and our shadow, although this can be challenging. It requires self-reflection because self-reflection allows us to acknowledge our inner complexity and strive toward personal growth. It also takes courage and honesty, as we accept both our light and our shadow. We need to accept both our inner strengths and weaknesses and acknowledge that our imperfections are an inherent part of being human.

I have only begun living in the fullness of the meaning of the contrasts of life in recent years. After living through many contrasting moments, I have come to believe it is important to appreciate life's contrasts so we can compare two or more options to identify the best option for us.

By seeing evil in the world, we can truly understand what good is. By seeing war and suffering, we can appreciate how good peace is. By knowing sickness and pain, we are grateful for our good health and well-being. Being in bad relationships makes us appreciate a good marriage or relationship. Comparing these life contrasts can help us be thankful for what we have, instead of complaining about what we do not have. In the real world, a good life is not immune to pain, stress, or adversity. A full life is lived through joys and tribulations.

If you meet anyone who says they have never been scarred by life, you can conclude one of two things: 1) They haven't lived long enough, in which case, they still have miles to go and will certainly encounter life in its fullest expression, or 2) They have lived in fear of risk, even the fear of expressing their own gifts because they are afraid of being judged.

As someone who has been personally and collectively affected by historic events I've experienced, I am constantly reminded of life's contrasts. For example, I can be joyful one minute and the next feel overwhelmed by guilt for living a blessed life when some of my fellow humans around the world are suffering, have little, or live in war zones and refugee camps. At some level, many of us have this type of guilt, especially when we are aware that not everyone is as blessed as we are. By our very human nature, most humans are compassionate beings.

Many of us are bold enough to envision a better world—one where divisions based on differences are completely rejected, and where uplifting those facing adversity is our highest priority. There is no need to feel guilty because we are blessed or privileged. Feeling guilty is not going to change the world. We must learn to appreciate life in all its contrasting moments and channel those contrasts into something greater than ourselves, like being kind to one another. In a more practical way, life's contrasts give us permission to act, confront the bullies, and use our voices to fight the world's inequities, and at the same time, kick back and relax with our loved ones and enjoy the view. We cannot skip this important aspect of life. We need to enjoy God's creations and the world's wonders.

Since you can't get out of life alive anyway, you might as well enjoy the living! And since you can't give what you don't have, making sure you take time to enjoy the big and small pleasures of life will enable you to fill your love tank, so you have more love to give others.

In all you do, always fill your love tank first; then give out of the fullness of your heart, not from an empty or half-full but a full tank of love. You can't give what you don't have, can you? When you feel the fullness of love with gratitude, go ahead and bless someone else. Most importantly, give without wanting to control the outcome, for you never know whose life you may positively impact, and who may influence yours. We are all wanderers through life, and no one has it all figured out.

Life's contrasts also apply to the quest for acceptance and a sense of belonging to a community, while at the same time needing space for individual expression. (As I shared in Chapter 1, there is no perfect social system.) This contrast can be found in evolved societies that have learned to balance individualism and collectivism. They have come to understand, since life is both about giving and taking, that life can only flow if people and societies are open to connections, yet confident enough to stand on their own. In this way, independence is achieved and, even better, superseded by interdependence.

However, this type of interdependence can be challenging to achieve for societies that are only individualistic or collectivistic. As much as collectivism could be praised in terms of social connections, we also need some individual thinking to challenge the status quo. Furthermore, your tribe, the community you belong to, may be found outside of your initial group. You have to make sure you create a culture of inclusion to expand your tribe and include anyone who understands your diversity and inclusion mission and is willing to lend a hand to promote it.

Nowhere else is the contrast of life more vividly expressed than in our human experience. Good exists alongside evil, and to combat evil, we must promote greater good in the world. Joy and sadness live nearby, so if we want more joy, we must learn to accept moments of sadness. And we can't appreciate order if we never experience chaos. These dual forces are all paired in a cosmic dance; we must inhale to exhale.

To achieve a higher consciousness, we must peel back the layers of our human complexity and move from unconscious to a conscious mindset. The contrasts of life allow us to prioritize community connections, but at the same time, to encourage individual accountability and creativity, and to move from a bystander mentality to actively advocating for a better world.

# CHAPTER 3

# Race in America: The Elephant in the Room

In my native language, Kirundi, we have a saying: "*Ibuye riserutse ntiryica isuka*," which translates to "When a rock is on the surface, it cannot hurt your hoe."

In other words, you can avoid hitting a rock when it is on the surface where you can see it. A hoe is the main tool used in most African countries to till the soil for any type of farming. While this saying has an agricultural context, it is profound enough to apply to almost every aspect of our lives. When something potentially harmful or troubling is no longer hidden, you have two choices: 1) Ignore the situation, or 2) Choose to change it.

Many of us may prefer the first choice, hoping the problem will go away by itself. Unfortunately, in many cases, this choice will not yield good or lasting results. The situation will only fester and become more troublesome. Ignoring the situation may be tempting because it involves no action on our part; it is passive. However, it is also very ephemeral, and sooner or later, the problem will most likely resurface.

The second choice is to act to change the situation. To achieve that change, you need to have a change plan. You need to identify what you can change in the situation and how you can alter it in a way that will yield positive results that will last, not just for a moment, but for a lifetime. If you choose this option, you will need allies who can help you achieve the goal.

Racism in the United States has become like the "rock" that can no longer harm your "hoe" because it lies on the surface. However, it will only remain harmless if we take significant action to change the course of racism in all its forms. Sometimes, when I am watching the news or listening to different reports and interlocutors speak about race issues in America, I realize people agree on something. They agree that racism is deeply rooted in the American collective conscience, whether we admit it or not. But, for whatever reason, people still want to have a debate about it, instead of meaningful conversations that can bring people together to dismantle racial discrimination.

In recent US history, we have seen different kinds of protest movements. We have also seen little or no tolerance for people's differences, whether they were about race, religion, or politics. If you have ever heard me speak or have read any of my books, you know I judge people by their individual behaviors and not label them based on their race or other sociological constructs. At least that is what I am trying to do. Whether you're black or white, or any racial identity, we all have a part to play in healing racial wounds—and that starts by healing ourselves. We are collectively to blame when race issues surface, just as we should collectively be praised for the good results we get when we choose good leaders who work to unite rather than divide people.

In these globally changing times, when all things are considered, it is hard not to see ourselves in the leaders we choose when we go to the voting booths. Although some exceptions exist, we usually vote for someone whose beliefs match our own. And when our politicians let us down, we are disappointed, even though we elected those leaders because they reflected who we are and how we perceive ourselves and one another. Then, not only is our personal leadership at stake; it is in crisis mode.

Schools rarely teach that true leadership is different from the position you hold. From a young age, I was taught that leaders were only those in politics or high corporate and organizational ranks. There was very little to no education about the importance of personal leadership and personal accountability. I hope that younger generations can learn these values and incorporate them into their formal education. According to many psychology experts, your emotional intelligence, also known as your EQ, is as valuable as your IQ and an important component by which your personal leadership should be measured. Someone might be educated at an Ivy League college or a prestigious university, but if they have never learned how to work in teams or learned the importance of having integrity and ethical behavior, they will fall short of their leadership potential.

Good personal leadership stems from self-love. I know self-love can be misunderstood or misplaced. In most cases, if we are honest with ourselves, we will find some underlying issues we haven't yet taken the time to work on, and we need to do that work to heal our wounds. Self-love comes mostly from acceptance—both self-acceptance and accepting others for who they are. As humans, we all crave acceptance. We all have areas where we need to grow both personally and professionally, and in which we should be growing and improving our lives. This also means taking responsibility for our growth and not blaming others for our lack of accountability and maturity. We should thrive on changing what we don't like, but we also need to know what we cannot change —including and especially other people's behavior. Knowing what we need to and can change, and having the grace to acknowledge what we cannot change, is leadership maturity.

Healing racial wounds starts with self-love, and once you learn self-love, you can help heal others and fight racism and other types of discrimination. When you love yourself for who you are, you don't hold hatred against your fellow humans just because they are from a different race, practice a different religion, or have a different sexual orientation. Self-love also allows you to forgive yourself for what you have done or failed to do, and to forgive those who hurt you, even when they don't deserve it. Why? Because when you love yourself, you will want to let the poison of hatred out of your system. Nelson Mandela said it best, "Resentment is like drinking poison and then hoping it will kill your enemies."

When you love yourself, you don't have the time or energy to bully others. When you love yourself, you become kinder and gentler; you are overtaken by feelings of gratitude, and you can't help but share that feeling with others. Therefore, it is important to love yourself from the inside out. It will boost your energy level, free your creative and innovative mind, and allow you to have more love for others. Loving yourself helps you create a constant love energy renewal and more peace of mind and soul.

In my book *Evolving Through Adversity*, I wrote a chapter about my journey to North America and my experiences as an immigrant woman adjusting to a new country and new culture. That chapter was born out of my confusion and sometimes utter frustration. I watched on the news how black people were treated, especially by the criminal justice system, and I saw how much race in America has become the big elephant in the room that people want to disappear. I realized the root causes of racism were not being addressed in meaningful conversations, from fear that those conversations might be uncomfortable or lead to change. And not many people like to be uncomfortable or change. The prospect of change creates an underlying fear of the unknown. But there is also an unwillingness to act on what we know is right. Out of fear, we choose to avoid race conversations or just downplay racial issues with the same old thinking that gets us nowhere when it comes to race matters.

In American society, we love to use labels for everything. While labels may help sort things out, they can intimidate those who, even though they are not threatened by race issues, could become allies in fighting racism. I have had people ask me if it is appropriate to say the word "black" when talking to a black person. Or they ask me to tell them the right term to use when referring to black people. "Should I say *black*? Or is it *African American*?" they ask. I once had a conversation with a white woman who wanted to know why her son told her she couldn't say the word "black" when referring to one of the boys on his basketball team. Her son told her, "Mom, it's inappropriate to say that word." She said her son's coach had told them that saying "black" was offensive.

I am not completely sure why people think the word *black* is offensive, but I think they confuse using that word with being racist. Most people think that if they don't use the word *black*, they don't see color. To them, not seeing skin color or race means less chance of offending black people or appearing *racist*. When it comes to race, the notion of being color blind is actually more offensive than not, because, like everyone else, black people want to be seen and heard. When someone says, "I don't see color," it translates to, "I don't see you; you don't matter to me." Why would being called *black* offend someone who is indeed black? What I think would offend is if you called someone something they are not. For me, since I am black and have been my whole life, I have no issue with being identified as such. To make my point here, I asked the woman, "Would you be offended if I said you are white when you are indeed?" It makes no sense to me. Events like these prompted me to become a diversity advocate so I could share what I know when it comes to racial differences.

We all have our social identifiers, but they don't make us good or bad, strong or weak, smart or dumb, rich or poor, pretty or ugly. They are just identity constructs. What gives words their relevance is the context in which we choose to use them and our intention in doing so. We can use them to denigrate or elevate, to build or destroy, to move forward or backward. The choice is all ours.

Understandably so, because of historic racial tensions, people want to avoid this sensitive topic; they hope that if we don't talk about it, it will fade away. But if we never address the elephant in the room, that doesn't mean it has exited the room! It is still there, hidden in our socioeconomic, criminal justice, and educational systems. And it is okay if you don't know the language to use when talking about different people. That is different than choosing not to engage with people of different races at all.

Ignoring can mean dehumanizing them in the same way as people who call them names. Not teaching the appropriate language to children is also how we create an imbalance in our society. It builds a psychological block where there is an *us* versus *them* mentality. Therefore, parents, educators, and leaders need to learn how to communicate with people and about people of all racial backgrounds, and teach that communication to their children, their students, and their colleagues in the workplace.

Most of these issues happen in our unconscious minds, and that is why, in this book, I want to share insights to help people move along the awareness stages (as I mentioned in the introduction) away from an unconscious mindset to an advocate mindset.

Instead of making assumptions, ask questions. Be curious and listen. Listen to those who go through the adversity of being denigrated, called names, and denied because of their racial backgrounds. Ask them how they are affected and how you might help. Therefore, it is important for government agencies—from the local to the highest institutions in the land, and for corporations, educational institutions, nonprofit organizations, and community groups to have a diverse workforce from the top leadership to the bottom floor so they can tap into that diversity of thought and ideas, leadership, and teaching and learning styles.

It took me a while to understand why anyone would ask whether they can use the word *black* to identify someone who is black. But it showed me where I was making mistakes. I realized that just because I had the opportunity to meet people of diverse racial and identity backgrounds, I couldn't assume everyone had. For example, I have met people who had never before seen or been near black people; it reminded me of some of my earliest memories of seeing white people in my native country, Burundi, when I was a little girl in the 1970s.

One such memory was when I started attending Catholic masses on Sunday with my aunt. The priest was a German named Henri Bonn, who was the head of the diocese in the south of Burundi. Whenever he visited my church, he held Mass in the local Kirundi language, which he spoke fluently with a huge accent. Later, when I started primary school, I frequently saw Belgian nuns who ran the hospital near my school. And because of Burundi's colonial history (colonized first by Germany and then Belgium), missionaries had come from European countries since the 1800s to help prepare the country for European colonization. This happened not just in Burundi but in many African countries. Many of these missionaries stayed even after colonization ended. It was also not uncommon to see white healthcare workers, so I saw white people early on, either in church or in medical centers.

Although it is hard to understand how people in the twenty-first century may have had no contact yet with people of other races, I understand that they may just not have had the opportunity. This is what awareness is all about. I also realized that just because I had experienced the *black experience,* which, by the way, is different from the American black experience (as discussed in the next chapter), I couldn't assume that every other person was equally comfortable with being called black. I tried to be open to learning where this person or that person might be coming from, and I tried to be slow to judge and not label people.

Furthermore, I understood that my way might not be everyone else's way of dealing with race issues. To stand with others, you may also have to be comfortable standing up for what you believe in alone. I have met some black people who have no tolerance for someone who would ask whether to call a black person "black" or "African American." I realize we all act out of our personal stories and journeys, and people may be offended differently, depending on where they come from or how they have addressed their own self-identity.

For example, asking two black people, "Where are your ancestors from?" might get you two different reactions based on the black person's roots and how they have healed their own racial wounds. One might feel you are reminding them of slavery, while the other might not mind sharing their roots. You just never know, and so, instead, learn how to connect using your own story. For example, you could raise the issue by sharing your own American immigration story, telling where your ancestors came from. It might seem like it's small talk, but it is a good way to connect with people of different backgrounds.

We also need to understand that adversity can happen to anyone, one way or another. Being white or of any other racial background doesn't prevent anyone from facing challenges. However, we also need to acknowledge that some black and Hispanic minorities in the US face significant hurdles when it comes to economic opportunities than the average white person. The best way you can use your story and your experiences is to enlighten those still afraid of differences and try to offer them the grace of learning what they don't know, should they choose to learn.

When we talk about racial problems, we often skip an important step, which is healing our personal and collective racial wounds. I have been in many a discussion on racial equity where the discussion turned into a debate or made white people feel guilty or defensive, and people of color feel like victims.

Shaming, or fear and guilt-oriented discussions, rarely yield any good outcome. Instead, people withdraw physically or become emotionally closed off. The cost of leading with fear of those who are different is much greater than the cost of including them. How do we replace fear with empathy and love? By going back to the basics of the true essence of who we are, and by acknowledging each other in our good and bad times. But why? Because, at our very core, we all want to be accepted for who we are, even if we might act otherwise.

Regardless of race, culture, ethnicity, religion, sexual identity, political affiliation, and diversity of ability and age, we all have the intrinsic yearning to connect with our fellow humans, to love and be loved, and to learn and grow. We all have dreams and desires we want to manifest on this side of heaven. Simply put, we want our lives to matter. I hope that we can evolve through the adversities of division and bigotry and forge long-lasting connections built on empathy and belonging.

As I shared in a TEDx Talk, "We Are Not All That Different," *the victim and the perpetrator are both wounded and need healing.* [4]

If we want to achieve real racial equity, we need to:
- Move from the victim mentality to an empowered mentality.
- Address the root causes of racial inequities and deepen our analysis of the origins of racial oppression so we can understand how our personal experiences and feelings about race fit into the larger picture.
- Stay open to differing perspectives.
- Raise awareness of the importance of operating not from a place of fear, but from embracing diversity and inclusion.

- Move from defending our privilege to acknowledging it, and most importantly, using privilege to come together as a community and fight for racial equity.
- Move from a "them" mentality to an "us" mentality by planning together, listening to one another, and learning and growing together.
- Channel our healing energy to heal each other's racial wounds.
- Overcome internalized inferiority or superiority complexes and shift from the oppressed or oppressor mindset to an advocate mindset.
- Understanding that dealing with uncomfortable topics is how we learn and grow personally and professionally.

For all this to happen, we must engage with people of different races and cultures; then we can recognize the disparities in privileges and disadvantages, learn what other people go through, and discover how we can support their journeys. In the journey to improving race relations, we need to begin within ourselves and heal our own wounds first. It is the only way we can heal our families, communities, countries, and the whole wide world. Only then can we heal from our racial wounds and push the elephant out of the room.

# CHAPTER 4

# The Black Experience

As a presenter, I have realized that any topic with "black" or "white" in its title can make some people uncomfortable. However, comfortable people rarely grow or become all they can be. As the elephant in the room, race is a timely and important conversation that needs to happen. But it seems like when broached, these subjects tend to send people into endless debates and defenses on the one hand, or some type of guilt on the other hand.

People who only cling to their own racial beliefs miss other people's insights, perspectives, and collaboration. This reality is not just for one race or the other, one political affiliation or the other, one culture versus other cultures; it is for all of humanity. We all suffer from what I call *humanititis*, my made-up word to signify our fallen human nature, also known as the human condition.

I was once asked to speak on race matters to a university class with a diverse group of thirty students or so, ranging from nineteen to twenty-one years old, from various racial and identity backgrounds. It was in the department of Africana Studies, and my lecture was on "the black experience." I wasn't sure how I could handle such a lecture, because, as an African, born and raised on the African continent, I knew my notion of race and what it means to be black was slightly different from those expressed by most African Americans.

Nevertheless, I accepted the challenge. Here is how I handled the lecture: Instead of assuming I knew what the *black experience* meant to the students and giving them a lecture, I set out to learn what it meant to each of them. I opened a conversation. The students were at first a little puzzled, and quite frankly, a bit shocked that, instead of just giving a lecture, I was asking them to be part of a conversation on race matters. I could see it was an uncomfortable topic for many of them.

I started by sharing with them my origins and my experiences as a black woman in my native country of Burundi, in East Africa, alongside many, many, many black people there. Here is what I said: "You know, in my native village where I grew up, people say I'm white."

When I said it, the students' facial expressions quickly changed. There was both shock and confusion. They looked at me, from head to toe, with their intense eyes, not really grasping what the heck I was talking about. To them, I wasn't white. Hello! Why would people in my native village think I was? But looking at the two African students in the classroom, I winked, and they smiled because they understood exactly what I was talking about.

"In my village," I continued, "people say that I'm a *muzungu* (or 'white person' in Kirundi, my native language). You want to know why?"

Thirty heads nodded *yes*.

"Because I wear nice shoes, nice dresses, and really cool sunglasses."

When I said this, the students exploded with laughter! As I continued to explain the reasons for my *whiteness*, I told them this mindset had been ingrained in many Africans' brains since colonial times. Because then, only white people were well off and could wear nice shoes, nice clothes, and cool sunglasses.

"And now, as an educated woman, I am well off compared to most people in my village, and therefore to my people, I am also white. The people in my village see no distinction between me and a white woman, and thus, my *black experience* and theirs are completely different, which is based on opportunity, and not only race or skin color."

After I said this, all the students in the room fell silent. I could see everyone was waiting for someone else's reaction to what I had just shared, and not wanting to be the first to show any emotion.

But my goal was to have a conversation with them, not give a lecture. I wanted to open their minds and share that the black experience is based not only on how each person perceives black people, but also on lived experiences, whether you are black or not.

I started asking the students to share their own black experiences, regardless of their racial backgrounds. One by one, I began to see a show of hands. The students started either to ask me questions related to what I had just shared or to share their own black experiences. I will never forget what one white, female student shared. She was so emotional as she said that, as a little girl, her parents never let her near black people. She wasn't allowed to play with black kids, and she attended a school where there were no black students. Her mother had even warned her that black people were bad people, so she grew up with this psychological message that she perceived as, "If you're black, you're dangerous."

I asked her, "What made you want to take this Africana Studies class?"

She said, "I always wondered why my mother never let me get close to black people, and so, when I applied for college, I wanted to go to an HBCU (Historically Black College and University) where I was sure I would meet black students." She said, adding,

"But when I met them for the first time, I felt awkward around them; I didn't know how to interact with them. I took this class to learn more about black history and African studies. And so far, I have best friends who are black, and my good grades are in black history studies."

I applauded this student not only because of what she had overcome in terms of racial bias, but also for being courageous enough to pursue the truth and rise above what her parents taught her about black people. And sharing her story with her classmates was another courageous act.

A white male student said his black experience came from the media's negative portrayal of black people. During that lecture, many students—blacks, whites, Hispanics, Asians, biracial, and students whose parents were immigrants or came as refugees—all shared something about their black experience in America, and in their native countries or cultures. The room's atmosphere went from tense to relaxed and communal. The students felt at ease with each other and me as they shared their black experience based on their own experiences and perceptions.

That day, the students taught me and each other a lot about how people, and especially young people, perceive the black experience. The students got a high score for participation, and I realized how much we needed these conversations on race in our schools and communities. We need to open spaces where students can explore their own identities, those of their classmates, and even those of their educators who might be different. This exploration, I believe, will enable connections and reduce the feeling of loneliness for young people. It will also broaden their sense of self-identity and raise their consciousness to know more about the world they live in.

I often ask myself: Why do we still have a hard time solving race issues in America? And why is race such a sensitive topic in our individual and collective psyche?

I believe most people want to end racial discrimination, but what we lack is the courage and willingness to confront the elephant in the room and end racism once and for all. We know what needs to be done, but it can be intimidating to do it, beginning with having deep and meaningful conversations about race, working together to end systemic injustices, and righting the wrongs. Even those who attempt to talk about race in the media have debates rather than real conversations.

The thing I don't like about debates is that there must be a winner and a loser. Debates and controversial TV might earn viewership and popularity, but it is not going to solve our societal issues. When using television platforms, we need a better approach to solving problems such as race matters in America because all debates accomplish is block the flow of conversations and the reflections ultimately required to heal racial wounds. There should be no winning or losing when talking about racial issues.

If done right, it should be a win-win situation. As humans, we sometimes try to dissociate from one another's experiences because we are afraid of our own biases and stereotypes. Often, when people feel lonely, they tend to lose confidence in themselves and others, and the byproduct of loneliness is disconnection. At the very least, we need to give our young people the space they need to talk about their black experiences without the guilt associated with the unfortunate events from the past, such as slavery and colonization.

I get that some white people have never seen a black person up close and personal. Yeah, believe me, I know this. I still get the "*Can I touch your hair?*" or people staring at me as if I were an exotic bird or something. I am here to tell you it is okay if you don't understand black people. It is all right if you haven't had a black experience. That is exactly your experience because no experience is also an experience. Therein lies the beauty of learning, asking questions, and seeking understanding about what you don't know. There is no need to feel awkward just because you have never met a black person before. And if you feel awkward, rise above your fear and take the opportunity to learn what you don't know.

Sometimes, during my presentations, people ask me, "How can I make black friends?" To me, that sounds like homework. And I hate doing homework. But I get it. Exploring new connections that might challenge your status quo can be intimidating. But making black friends should happen naturally, the same way you make any other friends. Be interested in what they do, where they live, and how they work and play—what makes them tick. Treat them as humans, not a project you have to work on. We are in this diversity experience together. Learn with them and from them, and let's go to the school of life together and uplift one another.

When I was writing this chapter, I came up with the acronym BLACK to help me (and whoever else might find it helpful) remember that being black is much more than just race or skin color. Here we go. **BLACK**:

- **B**e aware of the differences around you. Don't be color blind; be mindful of differences. Connect and build relationships with those you perceive as different and check your own biases and stereotypes.
- **L**earn what you don't know about black people—their experiences and how they live, learn, and play. Educate yourself about people's differences.
- **A**ccept yourself for who you are and accept others for who they are. Heal your wounds first. Love yourself for who you are, so you have enough love to give to others.
- **C**ommit to leading change with kindness, empathy, and understanding. Help create brave spaces where people can explore their identities and express their uniqueness.
- **K**now where to find different people and different cultural settings. The world is full of diversity; find it and enjoy it.

We all have our own black experience, no matter our racial background. When you approach race from a multicultural standpoint, you realize the black experience is much more than just race. It is a combination of psychological and socio-economic norms found in the complexity of people, systems, cultures, and subcultures.

# CHAPTER 5

# Working with Grandpa: Workplace and the Generation Gap

We cannot talk about unlocking diversity without talking about the challenges and opportunities of four generations working together. In one of my radio interviews, I was asked a question I have been thinking about ever since: "As a diversity advocate, how do you bring your message to those who might not necessarily be in tune with the perspectives you share?"

My perspective is that we are not all that different. In other words, we are more alike than different from an intersectionality lens. This interview came after my TEDx talk, "We Are Not All That Different: Race and Cultural Identity." [5]

That talk has resonated with many people, especially educational institutions and those who work with young people, because of the impact discrimination has on the youth. As I write this, for the first time in history, we have four generations in the workplace working together at this moment in time. These are the Baby Boomers, Generation X, Millennials, and Generation Z (or Gen Z).

On the one hand, we have a generation of Baby Boomers who are still working into their seventies. And on the other hand, we have Gen Z — fresh out of college and into the workforce.

Working with a not-so-young and not-so-technologically inclined boomer generation, the younger generations face both opportunities and challenges. They have different upbringings, different learning styles, different everything!

Even the conflict resolution styles are very different among the four generations in the workplace. And when you add to this mix cultural differences, then you have a simmering situation.

Whether we like it or not, millennials have been the generation that brought the most change to the workplace. For example, reporting sexual misconduct, demanding more equitable management practices, and asking for more work-life balance. And because this millennial trend will continue with newer generations that enter the workplace, management styles must evolve with the changing trends or face the consequences of being rigid.

## Some of the challenges of the generation gap
### Pressure on families:

This trend creates pressure on the younger generations to prove themselves, working long hours and feeling like they have no life. Families are put to the test, leading to frustrations and even divorces, late marriages, or no marriages at all, and as a consequence, fewer couples want to have children.

No one benefits when the workforce is frustrated, and employee morale seems to get worse every year in America.

### Quiet quitting:

The term *quiet quitting* started in 2022 and was cited by different sources as being made popular by a member of Gen Z who was a career coach. The term was meant to identify young workers' feelings of being overworked and burnt out, and doing minimum work, just enough not to get fired. Instead of demanding better work-life balance and mental health conditions, workers chose *quiet quitting* as a response to toxic workplaces where they felt overworked, not supported, and underappreciated.

They felt the management didn't care about them or their well-being, and they saw no channel of communication to voice their concerns without the fear of retaliation. A 2018 study from Office Team reported by Forbes.com looked to uncover the power of appreciation and found that "66% of employees would quit if they didn't feel appreciated." [5]

That number was found to be even higher for younger workers, with nearly 8 in 10 millennials in the same study saying they would leave their jobs if they did not feel appreciated by their colleagues or leaders. Unfortunately, that trend has not improved today.

Even in the remote work era, millennials are the biggest cohort in the workplace that seems to drive working trends. Therefore, there is a huge gap in satisfaction among employees of different generations due to the lack of appreciation by their leaders, most of them being from the older generations.

Additionally, the remote and hybrid work environments present unique challenges and opportunities that must be addressed efficiently.

## Boomers are starting to retire in big numbers:

As Boomers retire in big numbers, the good news is that younger workers will have more job opportunities to choose from. However, one can wonder if the newer generations are well-equipped and prepared to take over more senior executive positions. Since Millennials will be the majority of the workforce for the next decades, how will they shape the workforce and economy?

In addition, Baby Boomers made more money during their working years than younger generations are making, which in the US will affect how programs that depend on workers' contributions, such as Social Security and Medicare, will be funded.

It is not that younger people do not like to work; they simply do not save as much money as boomers did at the same age. This is primarily due to inflation and the rising living costs, coupled with the hefty student loan debt that many graduates face, especially those who attend universities and colleges in the US.

## What can we do?

First, we need to acknowledge that there is no one-size-fits-all model. Organizational leaders should take into consideration the diversity of the markets they want to serve and build a workforce that is representative of those markets. Second, employees need to feel that their leaders genuinely care about ensuring safe working environments where they can thrive and innovate. Third, organizational leaders need to invest in employees' self-motivation, have open communications with them, and listen to solutions that stem from those issues. Now, these solutions might cost money and resources, but the cost of doing nothing will be greater.

For the younger folks entering the workforce: Take the time to learn how older generations work, be teachable, and improve upon what you learn. Most of all, enjoy the process.

For more experienced workers:
- Mentor those who need it, especially millennials and Gen Zs.

For management:

- Build a work environment that is inclusive and welcoming. To avoid costly mistakes later, invest in your employees' understanding of who they are.

Matching employees' natural talents and skills with a position that gives them a sense of purpose will help them have a passion for coming to work. In addition, treating your employees like the whole human beings they are — and not as fragments that you work like robots pays off.

When you have a mix of generations and backgrounds in the workplace, everyone brings unique perspectives and ways of being, doing, and learning. In return, the whole organization benefits.

## Feminism and the generation gap

Is it *"getting harder to be a man than a woman"*? Young men's attitudes toward feminism.

As I was writing this chapter on the generation gap, I came across an article that discusses the gender gap in attitude toward feminism among young people (16 to 29 years old, which is Generation Z). The survey was done in the United Kingdom (U.K.) and asked males and females how they view feminism. Although done in the U.K., perhaps we can extrapolate some of its findings to the United States.

*"There's a clear gender divide in the attitudes toward the concepts of feminism and equality between the sexes, and the divide is most jarring among young people, according to a new study conducted in the U.K.,"* writes Josie Cox in Forbes [6]

In the survey, one in six respondents believes that in twenty years, it will be harder to be a man than a woman. Academics at King's College London's Policy Institute and the Global Institute for

Women's Leadership, in collaboration with Ipsos UK, surveyed 3,716 people above the age of 16 on their opinions and beliefs as they relate to feminism, gender equality, the barriers people face on account of their gender, and how these barriers are likely to evolve in the future.

## Falling under the assumptions

We may have fallen under the assumption that younger generations are progressive when it comes to feminism and gender equality. But according to this survey, they are not. Of people aged 16 to 29 years old, close to 65% of young men said that it was *harder to be a man than a woman*, especially when thinking about the future 20 years, according to the report. [7]

## Some of the key findings

"This is a new and unusual generational pattern — normally, it tends to be the case that younger generations are consistently more comfortable with emerging social norms, as they grew up with these as a natural part of their lives." [7]

Said Professor Bobby Duffry, the Director of the Policy Institute at King's College London. "This points to a real risk of fractious division among this coming generation of young — and the need to listen carefully to both (men and women)," he concluded. "That includes much more work on understanding the challenges facing young men today, or we risk that void being filled by celebrities and influencers." [7]

Professor Rosie Campbell, Director of the Global Institute for Women's Leadership at King's College London, agreed: "What we are seeing is a polarization in the attitudes of young men and women towards gender equality that matches the gender split…

We're just at the beginning of understanding what's driving this. But the fact that this group is the first to derive most of their information from social media is likely to be at least part of the explanation," She told reporter Josie Cox. [7]

If young people are more in tune with social media influencers who explain feminism in a way that might perpetuate misogynistic views, for instance, or those who reinforce gender role stereotypes, then this group might be getting confusing information or even toxic information about feminism.

The survey also found that: "Overall, just over four in 10 respondents said that they thought feminism had done more good to society than harm, while only 12% indicated that they thought it had done more harm than good."

So, that's good news, I guess. But still, having only 12% think that feminism has done more harm than good is not good. Shouldn't we be ahead of that? Shouldn't we be zeroing the divide on feminist views? I would have liked to see the research go further and find out what those who said *it was harder to be a man than a woman* meant exactly.

## Raising the next generation of feminist leaders

Gen Z is the next generation of people who are going to shape our modern world. When I read this article, it got me thinking. I wanted to understand why Gen Zs are thinking this way. Some of the questions I asked myself were: *Is feminism being misunderstood by the younger generations? And is there something wrong that older generations are doing in furthering feminism?*

Feminism has evolved, and feminism today is different from the feminism of the 60s or 70s. Explaining to younger generations what today's feminism is about is important to raise the next generation of leaders.

## It begins with redefining feminism.

Feminism is much more than just burning your bra (although that's also liberating). Being a feminist today is not just about being a woman or even fighting for women's rights. It is fighting for everyone's rights in all their intersecting identities and gender expressions, and acknowledging that not everyone is on a level playing field when it comes to fulfilling their needs. Giving women and men what they need to unlock their full potential is how we advance equity and inclusion. And we need more men to be feminists.

## Shifting cultural norms

I once gave a talk at a high school on the topic of bias and stereotypes, where I asked the students to share some of the cultural stereotypes and biases they have witnessed or experienced.

I remember one of the students — a tenth-grade girl — who shared that in her family and community, where her parents were from, girls were constantly told that they did not need to be good at mathematics.

She said: "That kind of messaging was internalized by my mother, and she never pressed me to do better in Math or Science, saying that *only girls who are not beautiful need Math or Science.*"

What the student said reminded me of my own culture of origin. There was little to no expectation for a girl to get good grades in math or the sciences. Parents who were progressive enough to even send their daughters to school wanted them to learn the basics. Girls were expected to be better in studies such as cooking, sewing, and other social skills than boys.

It is that social and cultural conditioning that made many women avoid fields that included math or the sciences. Although nowadays many women have made strides in STEM fields, the stereotype that *girls don't do Math* is still widely internalized — even in younger generations.

## Rolling with the times

Has the feminist movement lost its original mission? Or is it simply still misunderstood across cultures and generations?

Cultures evolve, and one can certainly ask if the feminist movement needs to change anything to catch up with the current times. The way feminism started may no longer be the way it needs to remain to benefit the next generation.

The previous generations did their part with what they had and knew at that time. Ending slavery and fighting for civil rights and women's right to vote are just a few of the many things the previous generations have achieved. Today, we stand on their legacy. But as younger generations discover their own potential to lead, they should realize that there are still some inequities in our systems and get involved in finding solutions to the most pressing issues of the current times.

Feminism is not about pitting men against women or raising women above men. It isn't even about women anymore. Feminism is about recognizing that all people deserve equal rights and opportunities. Gen Z must hear this message to lead us into a better era.

# CHAPTER 6

# Women and Work-Life (*Un*)Balance

### *You Can Have It All* – The best lie ever told

The older I get, the better I understand that the best lie ever told to women was that they *can have it all*. And by all, I mean a career they're passionate about and a family with kids to raise.

### Work-life balance is still more of a myth than a reality.

I used to watch a show called *Younger,* which is about a 40-year-old single mom who re-enters the working world after her divorce and finds herself on the job market. The problem is that she hasn't worked outside the house in more than 20 years, as she was a stay-at-home mom raising her daughter.

Now with her resume, the only jobs she could find were entry-level positions — competing with a younger demographic of twenty-something-year-olds who use abbreviations in their text messages. She then goes on to pretend she is 26 years old to get the job of her dreams. No spoiler alert!

I could relate to Liza Miller in *Younger*, played by Sutton Foster, and like her, I have asked what *IMO* means.

## An uneven level playing field

Let's face it, women with kids and men are not on a level playing field when it comes to working conditions. Regardless of identity background, if you have a stay-at-home wife who takes care of the kids and family, while you pursue and grow your career, and can travel the world for work, worry-free and guilt-free, that is a huge advantage many men have over mothers.

Yes, women have rights: they can vote, lead countries and corporations, or work in other positions, but they pay a high price for wanting to grow their careers. Many women who choose to work while raising a family feel the pressure and guilt of not being home full-time with their kids. Unfortunately, this is not just a woman's issue; it's a societal issue because it affects the whole structure of families and overall society. The COVID-19 pandemic has shown the disparities between the genders, and women who are mothers have been affected the most. Some of the disparities are due to the lack of childcare access, which has forced many working mothers out of the workforce.

And now the younger generations, mainly Millennials and Gen Zs, are delaying marriage, choosing not to have children, or simply choosing not to get married. One mom told me that when she asked her Millennial son when he plans to get married, he told her, "Mom, we have air-fryers now. No need to get married."

I said, "Wow! So now the air flyers are replacing wives?" I couldn't help but burst into laughter when my friend shared that with me!

## What can we do to achieve work-life balance?

Is it possible to level the playing field for working mothers? I think it's possible, provided that employers expand access to paid parental leave, as well as childcare and elder care.

In addition, organizations need to create better-paying jobs. For most women, especially working single mothers with young children, the cost of working often outweighs their pay and thus puts them at a sharp disadvantage. Some mothers choose to stay home to raise their families, but the downside is that employers don't usually consider staying home to take care of the kids as a skilled occupation, even though the managerial skills involved can be valuable. Do you know how well-organized and detail-oriented you have to be to care for a new baby? Or a toddler? Unfortunately, when mothers decide to go back to work after having taken time off, they don't have anything to show for their employment gaps.

## Supporting mothers to succeed in the workplace

It was always stressful for me to go back to work after having taken time off to have and raise my children. I remember some years ago, a recruiter who was helping me find a new job asked me, "Why is there a gap in your employment history? What did you do during all this time?"

I said, "I was home with my kids."

And the recruiter responded: "Home with the kids? Doing what?"

I wanted to say: "Watching *Barney, SpongeBob SquarePants, Bob the Builder*." I still remember the songs!

It is this type of scrutiny of women's employment records in a dismissive way that can lead to denying women employment. Or if they're hired, they're more likely to be paid less than someone who doesn't show an employment gap on their resume. As a mother, you may feel like there is no winning in the game of work and life.

Yes, some women have achieved career success, but they're often made to choose between career and family, and it can take a toll on their psychological well-being. Even in situations of remote working, women still pick up the heavy loads of caring for the kids and aging parents, in addition to taking on a lion's share of household chores. When it comes to generational gaps, Millennials (which is now the largest working demographic) are choosing to delay starting a family because they can see there is no work-life balance.

In September 2018, New Zealand Prime Minister Jacinda Ardern made history at the United Nations General Assembly by bringing her infant daughter. This was the first time a female world leader attended the forum with her baby, which many said was a symbol of a new era for working mothers and women in leadership.

However, as much as Arden's courage was applauded, that level of flexibility and leadership power is not afforded to everyday working mothers, nor is it the privilege even women leaders in other countries have. I can only imagine if an African woman leader had brought her baby to the UN assembly. Would she have been allowed to enter the forum? I am not sure!

In an article published by NPR, Ardern told *The Guardian*, "I have the ability to take my child to work, there's not many places you can do that. I am not the gold standard for bringing up a child in this current environment because there are things about my circumstances that are not the same." [7]

Arden was already a prominent public figure, serving as the leader of a developed nation. Bringing her four-month-old baby to the UN Assembly floor was a different kind of power, as she shared on the Oprah podcast: *Oprah and Jacinda Arden: A Different Kind of Power*, which aired on June 3rd, 2025.

When Oprah asked her what message she wanted to convey to the world, Dame Arden responded, "Yes, you can do it all, but you can't do it all alone."

Arden had also achieved many positive things for her country during her tenure as prime minister. Things such as extending paid parental leave for single parents, increasing government support for parents raising children alone. It is easy to view her act of courage as that of a typical working mother, but as she acknowledged that she had a supportive village to help her as a working mother, including her partner's support in raising their baby, which allowed her to focus on her job. This is something that many mothers, even those with spouses or partners, do not have.

The key takeaway here is that Prime Minister Arden recognized that while she could bring her child to work— a privilege due to her political power and leadership position— it does not make her the ideal example for all parents. It's impractical for mothers to bring their babies to the office, and it's not enjoyable for the babies either. What would they do? Watch their mom type on the keyboard?

This underscores the necessity for workplace systems to understand that each employee's situation is unique, and what works for one may not work for another.

## Women and the myth of having it all

When women have it *all,* that means having a growing career and a child or children to raise. We're not even talking about having a social life — unless it's solely centered on their child. Even those women who are in a relationship with a supportive partner still need to make the trade-off.

While systems need to change and organizations improve their work/life balance policies, real change can only occur when all members of society engage in a cultural transformation and shift in mentalities. Some women have realized that *having it all* also means having all the stress of a demanding career and missing out on some of their children's tender years.

It's all right for women parents to have realistic expectations about balancing careers and family life. In addition, societal norms should change in support of both men and women. Even with system improvements, many women find that achieving both is often the exception rather than the norm. Therefore, it may be possible to have it *all,* but not necessarily *all* at once.

## Life is about choices –It's about give and take

Unless you have the best spouse/partner ever who supports you unconditionally in your career and family raising, there is no work-life balance. You have to give some to take some. If you give it all to one area, the scale will tip in the other. For instance, you may think that you can give 100% to your career and 100% to your family and live an equally satisfying life socially and emotionally, but it doesn't work that way. Not in

America anyway. For things to change for American women, social systems need to change. People need access to free childcare and eldercare, flexible work hours, and paid time off for maternity and paternity. Gender roles also need to adapt to the changing times, so that husbands and wives share all the household chores.

These are among the goals of the modern feminist movement. Until these systems change, for many modern women — especially mothers, the reality of having and pursuing a career and at the same time raising a family may be the exception and not the rule. You may be able to have it all, but perhaps not at the same time.

## Understanding Mommy guilt: what is it?

I recently learned about the term "mommy guilt," and it perfectly made sense for how I felt as a mother when my children were young. This nagging sense of guilt stemmed from my perceived inadequacy in juggling parenting responsibilities alongside everything else life threw my way. I often felt torn between wanting to be the best mother possible and managing my own needs and aspirations—especially when I returned to school or started my first job.

It is important to acknowledge that many mothers experience this feeling, and there's nothing wrong with you for feeling this way. Your feelings are completely valid, and you are not alone in your struggles to balance motherhood and other life demands. It is clear that despite all the workplace flexibility policies in the U.S., there has not been much progress in work-life balance issues.

In recent years, some fathers have begun to take on the role of stay-at-home parents. However, due to societal expectations surrounding gender norms, there hasn't been a significant cultural shift, and women still shoulder the majority of the responsibility when it comes to family caregiving. This has led to "*mommy guilt*," where mothers feel torn between advancing their careers and being home with their children. On the other hand, those who stay home may also feel guilty for not prioritizing their careers. Mothers also often experience a stigma associated with being a *good mother*, which adds to the stress of their already demanding lives.

Although to a lesser extent, some fathers who are stay-at-home parents may also face social stigmas. At times, they are perceived as merely "babysitting" — rather than actively parenting their children, which can come across as not working. Moreover, fathers who take care of their children are often praised with compliments like, "*That's so nice of you to help your wife with the kids.*"

This societal conditioning can discourage many fathers from fully engaging in full-time childcare. Men need to raise the bar when it comes to raising their kids. If you are a dad, please, don't ever say that you're babysitting your kids.

Many working mothers say that work-life balance is still a myth, just another hashtag. Therefore, supporting mothers to succeed in the workplace means providing them with flexibility to work schedules that can accommodate their unique situations. And that's one of the best ways to attract and retain quality diverse talent, while fostering gender equity and inclusion.

# CHAPTER 7

# Should Stay-at-Home Mothers Get Social Security?

### What is the opportunity cost for stay-at-home parents?

In writing the previous chapter on the challenges of work-life balance for mothers in today's society, I wanted to explore the broader implications of social support systems, particularly regarding what more can be done to support mothers.

I came across an article that states that *studies indicate that there is an opportunity for stay-at-home parents,* and debate whether these parents should receive social security and other benefits.

I met a woman at a leadership seminar in Boston, Massachusetts, and we started chatting about our work. I told her what I do, and then asked her, "What about you, what kind of work do you do?"

In a soft voice, she said, "I'm currently not working. I stay home with my kids."

I looked at her in shock, and I sensed that she must have felt my gaze. I was surprised that she would suggest she wasn't working simply because she was a stay-at-home mother. She had three children under 10 years old, including twins. If that is not work, then I don't know what is.

She reminded me of myself when I was a stay-at-home mother some moons ago — often downplaying my efforts by saying I wasn't working. I know many other stay-at-home mothers who say the same thing whenever they're asked what they do. If it doesn't come with a paycheck, many mothers feel they aren't truly working. For a long time, the work done by women mothers who stayed at home to care for their families was viewed as non-work and still is in many cases.

Therefore, as I write this book, the stay-at-home parents' work has no social security or any other benefits. However, recent studies are starting to acknowledge the significant contributions of stay-at-home parents in our modern society. Often undervalued, these parents provide more than just a paycheck. They ensure family stability and perform essential domestic and emotional labor — all while exhibiting significant leadership skills necessary for human development. However, as a society, have we changed our perception of what stay-at-home parents contribute? Or do we still merely regard it as a form of *"not working?"*

## What is the real value of unpaid work?

In a study by Beike Biotechnology, a company that focuses on research, development, and clinical application of adult stem cells and related technologies, researchers explored the time that stay-at-home parents dedicated to their roles and calculated the cost of outsourcing these tasks across 80 global cities.

"Being a stay-at-home parent, devoting your time to the care of the family is a uniquely challenging commitment that requires tremendous physical and emotional effort. Yet it's a role where the value of the work done is often not acknowledged or even measured." [8]

While the study outlined the costs of raising a family of four in a few major European cities, its findings included some major US cities like San Francisco, Los Angeles, New York City, Washington DC, Chicago, and Houston. The research found that stay-at-home parents spend over 150 hours a month on household tasks like cleaning, shopping, cooking, and laundry — as well as childcare responsibilities, such as transportation and tutoring.

## How much would it cost to outsource stay-at-home parenting?

The researchers at Beike Biotechnology also analyzed the costs related to outsourcing various tasks across different cities. The analysis showed that outsourcing parental and household responsibilities for raising one child over 20 years would be most expensive in Zurich, Switzerland ($1.09 million), followed by Basel, Switzerland ($1.01 million), and San Francisco, USA ($1 million). [7] They determined the total expenses by multiplying the hourly rates for each task by the number of hours dedicated to those tasks throughout a child's upbringing, which they assumed would span 20 years per child.

Dr. Emily Chen, lead researcher on the study, said: "In an era where work-life balance is more challenging than ever, the role of stay-at-home parents is indispensable. They not only contribute to the economy but also play a vital role in shaping the next generation and building stronger communities." [9]

## Who is more likely to be the stay-at-home parent?

While there are no fixed rules about who stays home when a child arrives, there are often unspoken expectations. Typically, there is an uneven distribution of parental responsibilities, with mothers frequently serving as primary caregivers. This arrangement often allows fathers to continue their careers without interruption.

According to the US Bureau of Labor Statistics, "Married mothers remained less likely to participate in the labor force in 2023 than mothers with other marital statuses. By contrast, married fathers remained more likely to participate in the labor force." [9]

Even when a child becomes independent enough for their mother to return to work outside the home, there is often a significant gap in her employment history. This gap can make it more difficult for her to find a job. Even if she can find a job, she is more likely to get lower pay.

## What should stay-at-home parents be paid?

The study by Beike Biotechnology highlighted the essential role of stay-at-home parents, and their research calls for policies that offer better support, including resources, childcare assistance, and recognition of these parents' contributions to social security and retirement benefits.

Picture this: After dedicating 20 years to raising your child or children, you get social security and retirement benefits for your labor. That would be a remarkable shift in how we care about our families. Just the thought made me go, *Wow*!

## What does this mean for the United States?

According to an article published by the PEW Research Center, "For American couples, gender gaps in sharing household responsibilities persist amid the pandemic." [10]

While this article was published in 2021 in the middle of the COVID-19 pandemic, the situation has not changed much today. Mothers continue to represent the majority of stay-at-home parents — even in two-parent households.

## Fewer women are willing to have children.

Unless there is a cultural shift in workplace practices, it may become less appealing to younger generations — especially young women — to consider parenthood, which can also have societal implications, if fewer women are willing to have children. That is why financial incentives — as the research suggests — can significantly offset the opportunity cost for stay-at-home parents.

Access to social security and other benefits would make stay-at-home parenting more equitable and contribute to raising well-balanced children. Couples should discuss childcare responsibilities and who will be the stay-at-home parent before the child arrives. They should also talk about fair compensation for the one who cares for the family, while the other parent works outside the home. And if both parents choose to work, they should discuss how to fund childcare and support each other's careers. The responsibility for child-rearing should be shared and not solely placed on the mother.

No matter how much artificial intelligence advances, raising a child is one of the toughest jobs — it is a role that deserves greater recognition.

What do you think? Should stay-at-home parents get contributions to their Social Security to offset their opportunity cost? And what other benefits do you think they should receive?

# CHAPTER 8

# Recognizing Privilege

People who try to understand race issues in the United States often ask about the term *white privilege*. This happened at a conference where I was giving a presentation, when I had just started working in the field of diversity and inclusion. I was presenting on the topic of multicultural diversity, and other presenters were speaking on different topics like diversity in the workplace. I was one of only two black presenters, while the rest came from other racial backgrounds.

I had just finished giving my keynote, and when it was time for questions, an audience member, a white woman (maybe in her early fifties), raised her hand to ask me: "What about white privilege?" That was a question I was not prepared for since I had only talked about cultural differences and not race specifically.

Suddenly, the room became very quiet. I looked around to see if anyone would volunteer to answer the question, but I only saw sixty pairs of eyes looking at me, eagerly waiting to hear my answer. Still fairly new in this field, I wanted to please everyone, and especially not offend anyone. I could feel the atmosphere getting a little tense and the audience still waiting, but I was not sure how to tackle the question. I was tempted to dismiss it, but instead, I asked the woman, "Can you please elaborate on your question a little bit?"

I didn't want to assume I knew what she meant by white privilege, even though I had an idea. I wanted to hear her explain her question so we could all be on the same page. And she did just that.

"Well," she said, "sometimes white people need to understand they have privilege, and learn how it impacts nonwhite people."

As she spoke, I could see that for many audience members, this topic was very uncomfortable, to say the least. However, despite the discomfort, I realized the audience also wanted me to answer the question. I, myself, felt the need to deconstruct the phrase *white privilege*. We must acknowledge white people who want to work alongside those who are racially marginalized, instead of dismissing them as having "white guilt"—another phrase I often hear when the topic of white privilege is broached. *White guilt* is a loosely used term to criticize white people for wanting to contribute to the racial healing process. I am reminded of the movie *The Blind Side* with Sandra Bullock. In the movie, one of her friends criticizes Bullock's character, Leigh Anne, for having adopted a black boy. They are having lunch when one of her friends says, "Leigh Anne, is this some sort of white guilt thing?"

This line makes me wonder: How can we heal our society if we are always so quick to judge or dismiss those who want to participate in the process? The question the white audience member was asking me was, no doubt, a brave question.

In answer, I said, "I think as a society, we need to reflect on what *white privilege* is, and perhaps redefine it in a way that gives it a purpose, and to do so with understanding, caring, and empathy for those who are affected. If someone has a privilege that comes from being born white, that in itself is not a problem. They didn't do anything wrong."

Then I added, "What makes it an issue is if white people feel that talking about white privilege means taking it away, and feel the need to defend themselves. We need to distinguish white privilege from white oppression. When someone oppresses someone else based on race, we need to call it what it is, and in my opinion, it's not a *privilege*. It's oppression and it's injustice. Oppression and injustice do not have race or skin color.

When I finished answering, I could feel the atmosphere gradually relaxing. People started to nod *"yes"* to what I said. I then wished I had more time to explore this topic that day because I could tell it was uncomfortable for many, but it was also exactly what we needed to explore to make breakthroughs in our diversity and inclusion conversations.

The woman who asked the question also seemed satisfied with my answer. Since then, I have had many opportunities to discuss this topic and many other topics related to diversity in different settings and with various audiences, both young and old. My observations have always been the same: We need to have a balanced view of what *true privilege* is. Having white privilege does not mean you are oppressing anyone. No doubt, oppression is still prevalent in our society, but we have to be careful and not confuse it with having privilege, so we can work on ending racial oppression.

I am not saying white privilege doesn't exist, because it does. A white friend of mine shared how one day at an airport security check, the officer found a knife in her purse. When asked to explain, she told the officer she had put the knife in her purse to go out and cut down some dumb signs that had been hung up on her street the night before. And when she got home, she started packing for her trip and forgot to take the knife out of her purse.

The officer said to her, "You know you can't bring a knife on the plane. So, what do you want me to do? Mail it back to your address, or throw it away?" My friend said, "Oh, gosh, please throw it away." She was relieved the officer was clement and offered these two choices, and no frisking or accusing her of being a terrorist.

She was stunned to get away without any problem. After she told me the story, we both commented on how lucky she had been because it could have turned out differently. Then my friend said, "Seconde, that's when I truly understood my white privilege." The irony is that the signs my friend used the knife to cut down were racist slurs that had been hung up in her neighborhood by some people. I am grateful to her for the advocacy work she is doing to fight for racial equity.

I understand white privilege is real, but we must also be mindful of its context. I believe real privilege has no race or color; it can only be experienced as a privilege when we use it to work on issues that don't affect us personally, in any negative way. In other words, if your white privilege can allow you to advance a cause, solve someone else's problem, or simply bless someone else, then that is true privilege. We are all privileged in some form or another, and some are more privileged than others. Some use their privilege to serve others, and some don't even know they are privileged because they are too busy complaining about their lack of privilege.

I have continued to reflect on what constitutes privilege and how to bridge the gap between those with more and less privilege.

If we go back to the basics, regardless of our race, every one of us has at least one privilege we can identify.

Race in America remains an uncomfortable topic for many, particularly when it comes to discussions about the term "white privilege," which is often used in ways that can hinder meaningful conversations and connections about race. For some white individuals, discussing white privilege can feel as if it implies taking away from white people to benefit other racial groups. In a setting where I wasn't expecting to hear it, one man said, "I don't understand why black people complain about racial discrimination. There is no racism since slavery ended more than 100 years ago. It's just an excuse to be lazy." I cringe whenever I hear people make these kinds of statements to condone oppression and other injustices committed throughout history, starting with slavery and colonialism, the killing of Native Americans, and then segregation, with the ensuing systemic racism, especially in the criminal justice system.

As I shared in Chapter 3: Race in America, avoiding discussions of race will not solve the problem of racism in our society. My goal in these reflections is not to blame racism on white privilege. We need to call out racism when we see it, but having white privilege doesn't equate to being a racist. Many people come from a background of privilege, white or not. Other white people might ask, "How am I privileged? I'm working my ass off to provide for my family, just like everyone else." Having white privilege doesn't mean that your life is always easy; it simply means your race or skin color is not one of the contributing factors to your difficulties, and most importantly, having white privilege doesn't mean you did anything wrong.

Therefore, we need to have a balanced view when it comes to race and other diversity matters, and we need to bridge our differences in a more tolerant and connected way, with a common purpose. As I shared in Chapter 4: *The Black Experience*, when people in my native village referred to me as a "white person" or *muzungu*, it didn't mean I was guilty of committing any wrongdoing against them. They think I have white privilege because I am more educated than they are, and my way of life is closer to those of Western culture than my native culture.

While acknowledging the realities of white privilege, we also need to come up with another notion of privilege that doesn't attach itself to only the white race, and we need to deconstruct the word "privilege."

I know it can be hard to change our ways or how we have always seen our social constructs. But we can only overcome the divisions based on race if we are willing to change our behavior toward differences. It is worth emphasizing that deconstructing privilege is not giving a free ride to oppression or other misdeeds committed by anyone against blacks, Native Americans, Hispanics, Asians, Jews, Arabs, or other racial minority groups, whether in the United States or elsewhere in the world.

An argument I often hear from some white people is, "Why am I being blamed for things that happened before I was even born?" The truth is that racism was ingrained in many people's minds long ago, and most of those people are no longer here. However, the psychological, economic, and social impact of racism didn't die with those people. It stayed in our socio-economic, judicial, and political systems. Is the United States the worst in this regard? Absolutely not! However, the United States is a special country, built by people and for people of all backgrounds, many of whom came from somewhere else, consequently making it a melting pot. The underlying racism was left in place a long time ago, and its varied manifestations in our society today fall on all of us. Thus, it is up to us to right the wrongs done by previous generations.

No one should blame our current generation for the oppression and injustices committed a long time ago. And most minorities understand that we cannot, and should not, blame every white person for racial injustices. What people of color want is for our current institutions to take accountability for the current wrongdoings in our criminal and social justice systems. And for white people to understand that when we are talking about racial biases, it is not to blame white people or take away the privileges they have. It is to raise awareness so we can all work together to stop racial injustices. Furthermore, white people should understand that a world where only a portion of the population has privilege does not benefit them in the long run.

This is not to say that because the United States is not perfect, it is not a good country. Because it is indeed a good country, but it can be an even greater country when all people are treated equitably without prejudice.

I believe it is because leaders have shied away from bringing these issues to the forefront in the past that we are still struggling with race issues today. To heal our communities, both individually and collectively, we need to be brave and dismantle racism and all other negative isms. Taking a neutral position might work for the short run, but sooner or later, issues of race will come back to the surface and hurt all of us, regardless of our racial background. Both the victims and the perpetrators of racism and other inequities in our world today are hurt. Therefore, we can say we didn't commit those prejudices, but it falls on all of us to fix what is broken in our educational system, government institutions, and diverse communities. We need to reflect on our individual and collective privileges and find ways to channel them into a common purpose.

The truth is, we all have some privileges we didn't have to work for or ask for. Some privilege is inherent to our birthright, or simply comes from those who came before us, and who fought certain wars and struggles for us to enjoy our basic human rights. Many of the privileges we enjoy today didn't exist fifty or one hundred years ago, and they may still not exist in many parts of the world. Instead of taking our privilege for granted, let's use it to uplift those who are still struggling in the areas where we are privileged. And even if you have privilege in one area, there are other areas where you may face certain barriers that come from bias. We cannot put every white person in the same box. Otherwise, there is no individual accountability.

By the same token, we also need to acknowledge the racial inequities found in the criminal justice system. Even though the law was meant to be fair, if those who are in charge of enforcing the law are biased against black people, they end up punishing them more severely than their white counterparts for the same offense. This is pure injustice and not white privilege. We should have equal punishment for the same offense.

I think calling it *brutal injustice* would take race out of the equation and instead help advance equity in the criminal justice system. A great example is how black men are treated by the police in some communities across the United States. If you are the parent of a young black man, you are more likely to be concerned about how your son might be treated by the police than if you were the parent of a young white man.

Now, while this situation benefits young white men, it is not their fault that the police profile their young black counterparts. It just means they were born into a justice system that doesn't treat all people equally. Therefore, white people need to step up to the plate and defend human rights and equal justice. Otherwise, in the long run, the burden of not doing anything about our criminal justice issues will outweigh the privilege.

Another area of privilege is gender identity. Men tend to reap benefits from having *male privilege*. Historically and in most cultures, men have been privileged by society when compared to women, which today affects the pay gap in the workplace, among other things. White men also enjoy male privilege more than their black male counterparts. Please know that I understand life is not always easy for every white man, but the fact that white men don't have to prove themselves at work as much as women or black people, who often have to work twice as hard for lower pay, is certainly a sign of white male privilege.

There is a built-in bias when appraising men's and women's work. Men's work ethic is not questioned as much as that of their female counterparts, and this situation benefits them on many levels of the corporate ladder. The bias is found in many industries and at all levels of job classification. The longer this prevalent gender inequity goes unaddressed, the longer workplaces will have to deal with the pay gap, promotion gap, and other gender gaps.

Because structural and systemic issues are created by people, organizational structures, and systems, they can only be corrected when we come together and right the wrongs. We must address these systemic issues of inequity and stop blaming our inability to change on racial or cultural differences. Being white does not get you wealth. However, it may help you out of some of life's burdens that people of other races are forced to deal with.

Therefore, white people are privileged simply because they may not have to face workplace biases when those biases affect people according to their racial backgrounds. As a society, we have to recognize our individual and collective privileges and work to support those who experience different hurdles, such as racial prejudice, because of who they are. I believe one can only enjoy one's true privilege when one uses it to advance issues that don't hold them back in any way. In other words, it is how you attach a purpose to your privilege to serve those who don't have the same privilege as you.

Below, let's explore some examples of privilege and the various advantages that come with it. The goal of this table is to support those with more privilege in the fight for the rights of those who are marginalized and less privileged. The truth is, if our society enjoys the same rights, it doesn't take away anyone's privilege. This is not an exhaustive list, but it gives an idea of some of the privileges we sometimes take for granted.

| The Privilege Inherent to Your: | Advantage |
| --- | --- |
| Being White | Being who you are, having your racial birthright serve you, and allowing you to avoid prejudices that affect nonwhite people. |

| The Privilege Inherent to Your: | Advantage |
|---|---|
| Being Male and Straight | You don't have to face gender inequity or homophobia, and you can freely live your life without worrying about those issues. |
| Having Freedom of Religion | Practicing the religion of your choice without apprehension. |
| Having Financial/Socio-Economic Stability | Being able to choose where and how to use your money and other symbols of wealth, and not having to worry about meeting your basic needs. |
| Being Physically and Mentally Able | Being able to use your body, mind, and spirit to master anything you want without limitations. |
| Having Democratic Freedom | Having democratic institutions that treat people equitably and support freedom of expression. |
| Being College Educated | Having access to a good education, the freedom to choose your field of study, and the opportunity for better-paying jobs. |
| Speaking More than One Language or Being Culturally Fluent | Expressing yourself in more than one language, belonging to different cultures, or being acquainted with different people from different cultures and backgrounds. |
| Being Young or Aging Gracefully | Being young and vibrant, or being old and wise, and using your life experiences to mentor and teach. |
| Freedom to Choose Your Marital Status | Having the freedom to marry or be in a relationship with whom you choose, but also the freedom to remain single if you so choose. |
| Freedom to Choose Parenthood. Also, Being a Child with Parents. | As an adult, you have to choose whether you want to have offspring or not. As a child, having parents present in the household gives you a balanced upbringing. |

**Table 1.** Examples of Privileges and Advantages Inherent to Social Identities

On the flip side, the above privileges can become hindrances if we don't acknowledge our individual and collective advantages and use them to uplift those who lack the privileges we enjoy. You have the free will to choose whether to use your privilege to serve good or to serve evil. That is another privilege: the privilege of choice. No one is going to force you to do anything with your privilege.

Before I end this chapter on privilege, let me bring some balance to it. Many black people have faced negative stereotypes and racial biases, both in America and elsewhere, for a very long time. Therefore, some have bought into the victim's mentality, probably because it was a way for them to cope.

When I first moved to the United States, I noticed that in some of the black communities where there was too much poverty and high unemployment, there was also a lot of self-hatred. Self-hatred is reflected in how black people treat themselves and each other in their communities. Many avoid this controversial topic in diversity conversations, but we have to address it if we want all communities to heal and thrive.

For example, years of socio-economic inequities have created racial disparities and made some black communities more vulnerable to black-on-black crime, and increased crime rates. We cannot have a conversation on racial equity and leave out the challenges experienced by some black communities across the United States. We need to reflect on how to end this issue. While black on black crimes may be rooted in racial inequities, overcoming those challenges begins with changing personal behaviors, valuing everyone's life, and stopping the killings in communities.

Moreover, because black people are impacted by racial discrimination in general, they also have been pitted against each other based on their skin tone, which has resulted in *colorism* prejudice. I remember when I had my first child in my native country, women would come to congratulate me, and the first thing they would check was my baby's behind ears to determine if she would be a light or dark skin tone, because when babies are born, they look mostly white.

This wasn't because those people were being cruel; it was their experience of how they were treated because of their own skin tone. Light skin is often favored over darker shades, and I have heard many similar accounts from individuals in various parts of Africa, as well as within Black communities in America and other regions around the world where people have darker skin tones. Unfortunately, I have also seen some parents favor one of their own children over another based on skin tone, favoring the light-skinned ones. This can create rivalry and even animosity between siblings. It is important to add that sometimes, light-skinned people also face prejudice from people with a darker skin tone. It is a vicious cycle that needs more awareness, so we can combat it.

I understand there are no quick fixes to these problems, and there is much more that needs to be done in those communities. Some of the solutions could be that first, we need to get an understanding of the root causes of the mindset ingrained in those black communities, and work to reduce the economic instability that often generates inequities.

Second, government institutions should invest in communities of color with educational and economic opportunities and provide them with resources to help increase their full participation so they can develop themselves and their communities. Along with education and economic investments, we need to have new and improved systemic policies that are more equitable. Third, companies and organizations should also pitch in and invest in poor neighborhoods and use their wealth to enhance lives. And fourth, we need to mentor young people in those communities, so they can break the cycle of poverty and violence.

And the problem of racial crimes is not just found in black neighborhoods; it is also prevalent anywhere that we have poverty and long-term unemployment, in any community of any country. If left alone without hope, communities end up turning against each other to survive. Therefore, systems and policies need to change and be more inclusive.

I am sharing these reflections because sometimes people get hung up on words like *white privilege* and forget the privilege of life, and that taking another person's life is not how we solve inequities in the world. Racism is rooted in systemic structures that benefit or discriminate based on identities. We can only correct implicit biases that benefit some, but not all people, by taking a reflective course. It is also important to secure our self-identity and confidence in who we are, so we can develop thick skin against some of the stereotypes, because we cannot control other people's actions.

When you know who you are, what your core values are, and what your life purpose is, it is unlikely you will oppress someone else based on their differences.

To join the conversation on race as an individual, it is important to ask yourself these questions:
- What do I want to achieve with race talks, and how can I create space for more people to join?
- How can I bring people together and, instead of widening the gap, bridge it?

- What are my driving values? What do I cherish?
- How can I become less defensive when someone else asks for the same privilege I enjoy?
- What programs can I invest in to empower underserved communities?

Being able to come to the table and work to end discrimination is not easy by any stretch. It requires all of us to use our resources, both financial and human, to share knowledge, perspectives, and, ultimately, a common purpose.

Here are some questions to consider during your team discussions or event interactions. This list is not exhaustive, so feel free to add your own questions. They can help spark conversations about how to use your privilege with purpose.

- How can you use your privilege as a white person to alleviate issues that negatively impact people of color and reduce racism and oppression?
- How can you use your privilege as a Christian to speak up on behalf of those persecuted because of their religious beliefs?
- How can you use your privilege as an educated person in a global world where education is not guaranteed in many countries?
- How can you use your privilege as a man to stand up for women's pay equity in the workplace or other issues affecting women in our society?
- How can you use your privilege as an American citizen to raise awareness of key issues affecting immigrants and help mitigate issues of racism and discrimination?
- How can you use your privilege as a person with an able body and mind to help those discriminated against

because of things they can't change, such as a disability (diverse abilities)?
- How can you use your privilege as a young person to help the elderly in our society?
- How can you use your privilege as a wealthy person to help eradicate poverty in America and around the world?
- How can you use your privilege as an immigrant to help educate schools, the workplace, and communities that don't have a global view of the multicultural world?

Early in this chapter, I said that we all have privileges in some areas, and we do. If you belong to a minority group, you may think you don't have any privileges. Let me stop you and say, of course you do! Go back to Maslow's hierarchy of needs that I shared in this book's introduction and see where you stand on the pyramid. Are your basic needs met? For example, do you have a shelter or access to safety and security? While you may not have too many privileges, don't forget some people don't have what you might take for granted. It's a matter of recognizing the privilege and using it to empower yourself and others.

It is also a good thing to remember that sometimes our privilege is in the form of a *gift* or a special talent we have. Aside from social and economic privileges, almost every person has been entrusted with at least one gift. We all have at least one unmerited favor we received as a gift, and it's up to us to choose to use it as a privilege to uplift or inspire our fellow humans.

Of course, if you have never experienced discrimination because of who you are, you may not understand what it is like. That is your privilege too, and you shouldn't feel guilty about having privilege in that way. But at the same time, don't be a bystander when you see bigotry around you. It may even be coming from your family members or the people you love. Put yourself in the shoes of those on the oppressed side of racism and other injustices, and ask yourself:

- How would I fare in that situation?
- What would I do if I were treated that way?

Then take some steps to ensure no one is discriminated against because of who they are, especially when discrimination is based on things they cannot change about themselves. That is what recognizing your privilege is all about.

# CHAPTER 9

# Embracing Cultural Integration

When I first published my book, *Evolving Through Adversity*, and was looking for ways to promote it, I came across an event where I could meet media producers from all over North America. I paid a substantial sum of money to attend the event to meet those media producers. It was an intense three-day summit, where I met producers from various media outlets, including some from major TV networks. I had signed up for this event particularly because I was looking to meet TV producers, pitch my message, and hopefully, expose my book to a wider audience.

On the second day of the event, I met with some TV producers. One was a female junior producer from a major TV network. I was so nervous, but I knew this was my big chance to pitch a show idea. After listening to me for about two minutes, the producer stopped me and said, "I like your idea, and I think your story has an audience."

My heart leaped with joy. Yes, finally, I had a shot to be on TV! Oh my goodness, I couldn't believe my ears.

Then she added, "But there is only one problem."

"Oh. One problem? What kind of problem?" I asked her.

"It's your accent," she said. "Unfortunately, with your accent, I'm afraid my network would never book you. I suggest you go back, take a few months to lose your accent, and then pitch to us again when you have an American accent." Then she turned away and called the next person in line.

Feeling overwhelming shame, I gathered the fancy folder I had purchased for the occasion and left. In my head, I thought, *"A few months to lose my accent? Oh, God, how am I going to do that? It's gonna take me at least seventy-five years."* I felt a rush of emotions and an urgent need to cry, so I went to the bathroom and wept. Then I went back to my hotel to deal with the rejection from all those media people. I felt so wounded. I had thought this was my chance to break through and promote my work on television. But I had to face the harsh reality that because I had a foreign accent, my work would not be considered.

As I thought about what the TV producer said, I entertained the possibility of working on changing my accent. But what do people do to lose an accent? And lose it fast? I felt I needed to research "How to lose your accent in ten days." Perhaps Google could tell me how to quickly lose my accent. (This was before ChatGPT). But I realized my accent wasn't going away any time soon. Obviously, I didn't change it.

And even if I could and wanted to change my accent, which American accent would that be? The producer didn't specify whether I had to change to a Southern accent, a New York accent, or a Midwestern accent.

But from that experience, I learned something. The first thing I learned was that cultural bias is lodged in our individual and collective minds. It may be dormant, but it is alive in all people, regardless of their background. Whether we are aware of it or not, we act out of experience. I don't know the real motive for why the TV producer didn't want someone with an African accent and felt my ideas were unworthy of consideration unless I spoke like the majority of Americans. However, I think her perspective mostly stemmed from the homogeneous environment in which she worked.

The second thing I learned was not to take it personally, and maybe even to be empathetic toward someone I felt wasn't being fair to me. Even though TV producers are in a position to showcase diverse people, cultures, and ideas, they may not have the power to bring in individuals who do not conform to the norms desired by their network's leadership. Producers might act this way because they don't want to challenge their network's status quo and protect their own jobs. If the network doesn't prioritize diversity and inclusion, especially among its upper leadership, why would a producer take a chance on someone with an accent?

## Cultural Assimilation: Is there an alternative?

As a newcomer to North America, one word I dreaded hearing was *assimilation*. This word was thrown around as if it were the only solution for all the problems immigrants were facing—especially regarding job opportunities. Immigrants were told that to succeed in their new country, they needed to assimilate into the culture. This obviously meant getting rid of our original cultures, values, and foreign accents to adopt the new culture we had come into. We needed to ignore the good in what we brought as immigrants and just assimilate. And believe me, many of us have tried, because we want to succeed, of course. However, many immigrants don't really find assimilation to be the solution to their many unique needs and cultural experiences.

The situation I had with the TV producer opened my mind to something about our human diversity: As immigrants, we don't need to assimilate; we need to integrate. Simply put, cultural integration means the majority and minority cultures can mix and mingle their cultural heritages, sharing without anyone having to give up the characteristics of their original culture. It also means integration of different ideas, where there is no subordination of one idea to the other, but a sharing in harmony despite the differences, which also means it's okay to disagree without tearing each other down. That way, we can celebrate the synergy between what is unique about our heritage and what is common in our diverse identities. And that is how I got into this work.

Instead of becoming bitter about the discrimination I faced as an immigrant, I chose to be better at educating myself and others about our differences, and I became a diversity and inclusion advocate. I wanted to help business owners, organizational leaders, and individuals have a broader view of themselves and others in the increasingly multicultural world we live in. I realized that having a foreign accent is an asset, not a liability, as the TV producer told me. It reflects that I can speak more than one language, and it is a strength in opening a window of business opportunities for those who have only lived in a homogeneous society or who don't have the privilege of speaking more than one language.

There is no need to assimilate to any one culture. What we need to do is take the best from each culture and work with that flexibility. In any case, who said there is a good and a bad accent, as long as you can get your message across? Now, I would be the first to admit my English limitations because English is not my first language, but reading and writing books and other content in English has helped me improve it exponentially. Now, here I am writing my fifth book in English.

I understand that there are countries where they speak with an English accent different from the American accent, such as the British, and in most cases, the British accent is considered "sexy" and not a problem when it comes to a foreign accent. But in most cases, speaking with a foreign accent means you can speak more than one language, can adapt to more than just one homogenous culture, and can process things with a diverse lens. What if the TV audience wants to see more people with accents in their favorite shows? People with accents also watch TV, you know. But I get that it might not be the TV producer's fault; the industry dictates it. I understood her dilemma and why she wasn't going to take a chance on me by presenting my ideas to her boss and saying, "Look what I found! An African woman with an accent to boot, yay!"

If we never see different people or hear different accents in the media, or in movies and shows, it creates shock waves in our brain the first time we do, and how can we feel comfortable with that? Unconsciously, there is a blockage. But if we start seeing and hearing people with different accents and racial backgrounds, our brains will start perceiving it as normal, and the shock will lessen.

I would say things have improved in some ways, especially in movies. After all, the Marvel movie *Black Panther* was a hit around the world, mostly because, for the first time, we saw African actresses like Lupita Nyong'o and Danai Gurira play lead roles and be portrayed as heroes in the movie that started the

"Wakanda forever" salute. Audiences around the world, and particularly in Africa, welcomed the movie's vision as the first Marvel movie with all-black leads, and it was the highest-grossing film in eastern, southern, and western Africa. The movie was shown in several schools, and for the first time, little black and brown kids all around the world could see themselves in those actors and dream of exploring their full potential, seeing possibilities instead of only limitations. You can't aspire to be what you never see. *Black Panther* spoke to the opportunities that diversity offers in any industry and the importance of inclusion. Its success tells me that the world is hungry to see more diverse faces on screen, hear diverse voices, and learn from diverse stories.

Over the last few years, although it still needs to improve, we have seen a slight increase in the representation of Africans on American television, particularly in sitcoms, talk shows, and lifestyle shows, underscoring the need for greater diversity on television. We must see people whom we can identify with, and who reflect the diversity of our modern society, doing good things, instead of only showing negative stereotypes. Now, with the increase of media streaming services, even people outside the US can watch American television. The media can benefit from creating inclusive cultures that harness the power of our diverse world and serve as a vehicle for solving social issues, such as ending discrimination and inequities from diverse angles. In 2019, during the fourteenth season of NBC's *America's Got Talent,* then twenty-two-year-old singer Kodi Lee, who was blind and had autism, won the competition.

When Lee came on stage for the first time, accompanied by his mother, who was helping him walk, no one expected what was going to come out of this young man's mouth. I cried as I watched him sing and play the piano; he was so good! We, as a society, would have missed his gift if he had not been given a chance to showcase his talent. Kodi Lee is a person with limited abilities in some areas but gifted in others. His example demonstrates that representation matters and can inspire hope for those who are underrepresented or disadvantaged due to their identity.

# CHAPTER 10

# Finding Common Purpose

It was early 2020 when the world was turned upside down by a global pandemic called the novel coronavirus (COVID-19).

During the pandemic, people were forced to isolate themselves in what came to be called "social distancing." This forced people to distance themselves from others physically; countries to shut down their borders; schools, businesses, and places of worship to close their doors; and even public places like parks and beaches to restrict access. The stock markets came tumbling down, and the New York Stock Exchange even temporarily shut down trading (something that had not happened since World War I in 1914) and moved to electronic trading. All these shutdowns and the enforcement of social distancing were done to stop the spread. Worldwide, the death toll rose into the hundreds of thousands.

However, during this worldwide crisis, we also witnessed the human spirit at its best. People mobilized to help one another, governments collaborated on the latest science and technology to fight the virus, and corporations and nonprofit organizations pitched in to manufacture medical equipment, including ventilators and masks for the overwhelmed medical workers. Some healthcare professionals came back from retirement to fill in for doctors and nurses forced into quarantine.

Although COVID-19 did not discriminate based on race, gender, nationality, political affiliation, or any other diversity dimension, some communities experienced more significant health and economic impacts than others. The pandemic revealed vulnerabilities in people and systems, depending on socio-economic status. Inequities in society resulted in hardships for the less affluent. For example, while some people could afford to work safely from the comfort of their homes on their computers, others had to work in potentially dangerous environments, such as medical workers and first responders, as well as grocery store employees, who had frequent contact with possibly infected people. While some people emptied the stores, buying food and cleaning supplies to hoard, others struggled to make ends meet, especially when the places where they worked closed, leaving them without a paycheck.

Due to health inequities in the United States, the virus affected communities differently, revealing sharp disparities between the rich and the poor. The well-being of a community depended on access to services; those with the least access to healthcare were the most severely affected. People with lower incomes had to rely on public transportation to buy groceries or attend doctor's visits, thereby putting themselves at greater risk. Communities of color, such as black Americans and Latinos, experienced the crisis differently because of the pre-existing economic hardships. They already lacked job opportunities with good pay and benefits, proper medical care, and housing equity that would allow them to live in neighborhoods with well-funded schools, which created a vicious cycle of poverty.

It is important to analyze the existing systems of inequality in order to understand their consequences. The coronavirus pandemic and the ensuing economic crisis altered everyone's lives. We had to reevaluate the way we work, shop, connect, and care for one another, as well as our aging population. The elderly and people with pre-existing health conditions were the most affected by the pandemic.

At the same time, many people were generous. It was as if the pandemic gave us a moment in time where we could stop and reevaluate our humanity, rethink and reshape our core values, and become more tolerant and united in our differences. Our shared humanity shone through in our care and consideration for one another in times of crisis. For instance, we witnessed the kindness of restaurant owners who generously offered free meals to those who were struggling and in need of food. The best and the brightest in the fields of science and medicine were encouraged to let their gifts and knowledge shine brightly as they collaborated to find the cure (or vaccine) for COVID-19. This is what finding common purpose in difficult times is all about.

Sometimes, it takes a crisis to bring people together, like the mobilization we witnessed in the protest against police brutality in May 2020. People were united in a movement to demand changes in the criminal justice system.

As you continue to demand justice, remember that activism is not limited to public protests, but extends to what you do after the protests. If you care about social issues and want to advocate for racial equity, how you continue the journey is much more important and difficult, too. It involves your willingness to fight for racial equity wherever you live, work, and play. How you treat your neighbor, coworker, student, educator, and others from different backgrounds speaks to your level of activism. It involves changing mindsets and working together with those who are affected to bring forth reflections and solutions to the unique challenges.

More than ever before, we need to work together on a common project and find a common ground—a project that will allow our children, their children, and their grandchildren to inherit a world where divisions based on differences are no longer welcome. A world where people can agree to disagree on politics, but not on the fundamentals of integrity and justice.

If we could come together during COVID-19 with a common goal to fight it, why can't we do the same with other issues? What about our gun laws and reducing mortality due to gun violence? Like race in America, guns are another sensitive topic people would prefer not to talk about. Yet they affect our country just like any other killing disease, the moment someone enters a church, school, or any public place and starts shooting.

When someone, for whatever personal motives or in whatever state of mind, opens fire on people, such a killer is not acting on behalf of Democrats, Republicans, Muslims, or any other group. They end up killing all kinds of people. As a society, we have three choices when it comes to gun violence:

- We can make it a political case.
- We can blame it on our differences.
- We can work to regulate guns in the safest way.

In the United States, opioid addiction and other forms of substance abuse are at an all-time high. In 2017, the White House commission charged with advising on the country's opioid epidemic called on the president to declare a state of emergency to quickly and aggressively address the opioid crisis. When a crisis like this hits our communities, it is not because someone is black or white, or of any other race or background. What we need to do in such crises is, as a society, look past our differences to help one another learn how to navigate life a little bit better so we don't end up destroying our lives and the lives of our children.

As I frequently share in my presentations, everyone goes through adversity in one way or another. How we respond to life's adversities is what makes the difference. Two people can face the same challenge but respond in opposite ways. Why is that? To me, such differences are fascinating. This fascination is what led me to my profession, and I embrace the journey of lifelong learning and thrive on uplifting others. I don't claim to have all the answers, and if you meet anyone who claims they do, run for your life! Because, truly, no one does.

The cause of differences in our response can be difficult to identify. Some say being optimistic or pessimistic could be linked to our genes. I am not a scientist or psychologist, so I don't know why people respond differently to the same event. In an imperfect world, we need to learn how to balance each other in our half-full and half-empty kinds of personalities. Even in the face of the coronavirus pandemic, people responded differently. Some collected household goods in panic, while others were slow to react and only bought what they needed.

How we respond to adversity is a conscious choice we must make. We are all on a journey of self-discovery on this adventure we call life. I learn from my life experiences and then turn around and share what I have learned with others. You may be facing some adversity right now that you don't know how to evolve through. As the saying goes, "When life gives you lemons, make lemonade."

Making lemonade is a figurative way of saying, when things are bad, look for the silver lining and make the best of the situation. And when facing adversity, try to build resilience. But what if you don't know how to make the darn lemonade? It is not always easy for many of us to make lemonade out of our lemons; it can be easier said than done.

I am often asked: "Seconde, how did you get started in this empowerment work?" I got started by using my story to teach what I have learned. Maya Angelou said it well, "When you get, give. And when you learn, teach." There is power in our stories, so I want to inspire people to explore the authentic power in their stories, regardless of race or cultural identity. But to see and use your authentic power, you need to move from the *why me* to *what can I learn from this situation* mindset. That way, you operate from a fear-based mindset to an awareness mindset.

We can use our pain and our story to bless others. In this way, our story becomes the fuel we need to be our best selves and do our best work. What we focus on will grow. The choice is ours. We all have free will to choose the kind of difference we want to make and the type of legacy we want to leave behind. My question is: How are you choosing to use your story?

As the world continues to change, we will continue to face complex problems that need complex and diverse solutions. And as Einstein said, "We can't solve problems using the same kind of thinking we used when we created them." Let us leverage our differences to enhance our ability to unite in finding a common purpose to address the world's inequities. Let us create a world in which diversity, equity, and inclusion are central to our personal and professional lives.

# CHAPTER 11

# Doing Business in a Multicultural Market

### What I learned about stereotypes and bias from a roofing salesman

One beautiful afternoon, I was home doing some work on my computer when I heard the doorbell ring. I immediately went to the door and opened it. A young man was standing in front of the door, and when he saw me, he asked me, "Is the owner of the house home?"

I looked at him, and I knew I had showered and was wearing my not-too-bad and not-too-good jeans — my mommy jeans. Discreetly, I patted my chest to check if I was wearing a bra; thank God I was. Because you know…working from home, there is no guarantee I'm going to always wear a bra. So, I looked acceptable in my opinion.

I said, "No, they're not home."

When he heard me speaking English, he looked me in the eyes and then said, "Oh, are you the owner of the house?"

I said, "Yes, I am. What gave it away?"

Then he launched into his memorized sales pitch: "We are replacing roofs in your neighborhood, and we have a special discount going on…"

In my head, I was like: Well, too late, buddy! You've already determined that I didn't belong in this neighborhood by your assumptions. But I didn't say anything to him. Instead, I said, "No, we don't need a new roof."

As he left to go to the next-door neighbor's, I wanted to shout at him and say, "Who's your manager? I want to talk to your manager!"

But of course, I didn't.

As I thought about what that young man said to me, I thought of how his lack of cultural competency might have cost him a sale, simply because of his assumptions that I didn't belong in my neighborhood, instead of being curious.

How many instances of conscious or unconscious bias like that have cost us opportunities, just because we assumed we knew what we didn't?

## Unconscious bias happens to all of us.

We have all been in situations where someone said something culturally insensitive that didn't sit well with us, like in the story I just shared about the roofing salesperson. Or we may have been the ones who said something without even knowing we were offending someone else.

A few years ago, when I was new in the diversity, equity, and inclusion field, I attended a conference where I met a black woman who was wearing a muslin hijab. In my attempt to connect with her, I asked her: "Are you Somali?"

She said: "Nope! I'm from Texas — born and raised in Dallas!"

I wanted to kick myself for my lack of tact.

Here is what I did: I immediately apologized for my assumptions, and she was gracious enough to accept my apology for my unconscious bias. I then asked her: "Do you get this question a lot?"

And she said: "You have no idea!" And we both laughed. We sat together in the conference room and became acquainted as we explored our differences and connected around our common ground.

Here is what I learned in that situation:

After I recognized my lack of tact in the way I asked that woman about her background, I had to ask myself these questions:

Where did my unconscious bias come from?

What did I hold in my consciousness that influenced my beliefs about myself and others?

And most importantly, going forward, how was I going to change and learn how to interrupt my unconscious bias whenever it acted out?

That's the work we all need to do. I can't promise that I will never make similar mistakes, but I can learn from each situation and do better next time. Now my motto is: Give grace so you can receive grace.

We all mess up sometimes, but the important thing is to recognize when you mess up and remedy the situation. The problem is that often people stop engaging or learning just because they messed up.

## So, how can we interrupt unconscious bias?

It begins within ourselves: by being secure in who we are and what we want to do. Interrupting unconscious bias comes from looking inside ourselves and discovering our values and what we stand for.

Looking at our blind spots: by not falling into the trap of: But, I'm a good person or I'm not a racist trap, and other excuses we use when we don't want to grow our mindsets.

What differentiates *conscious* from *unconscious* bias is the awareness of it and the intended results of our actions. Fortunately, unconscious bias can be overcome and disrupted by practicing self-awareness and increasing our consciousness.

We are flawed human beings, and we live in an imperfect world. As long as we are doing our best and learning what we don't know by asking questions instead of assuming, we can move forward and create a more inclusive environment that is welcoming.

According to the United Nations, in 2015, the United States had 48 million immigrants (foreign-born individuals), the highest number of any country.[11]

For centuries, whether due to voluntary or forced migration, people from around the world have made the United States their new home. However, today's immigration patterns and those of the past are different. Back in the nineteenth and early twentieth centuries, immigrants to the United States were mostly white and came from Europe.

Today, immigrants are mostly from Asia, Africa, the Middle East, and Latin America. Not only are immigrants to the United States different in their origins, but within the same country, they have different subcultures, classes, and different life experiences. One of the biggest mistakes people in the US make is assuming that all immigrants have the same story.

For example, when it comes to English, some immigrants come to the US already fluent; some are not fluent but manage to understand or speak a little English. Some came as refugees, escaping tyranny, while others may have come as permanent residents. Some immigrants may have been educated at private schools, while others may have never set foot in a school before or struggled to pay their school fees. Some came from well-to-do families, while others never saw a flush toilet (inside the house, people!). The point is, not all immigrants have the same story. It is important to meet them where they are and learn their cultural habits to do business with them successfully. And this realization is essential for all kinds of businesses, from large corporations to small companies, from educational institutions to nonprofit organizations.

When immigrants come to America, they still carry their baggage, both literally and figuratively. This reality has caused the art of business communication to evolve, and with these ever-growing migration trends come new purchasing power, along with different cultural buying and selling habits. In many African and Asian cultures, for instance, the price is only agreed upon after exhaustive negotiation. Furthermore, when people from these communities immigrate to the United States, they bring their cultural values and customs with them. American businesses need to learn how to do business with multicultural communities and avoid any potential unconscious bias that can prevent them from effectively interacting with customers and clients from diverse backgrounds.

## Overcoming Bias to Build Inclusion

In today's ever-changing and competitive business world, with ever-growing diversity among people and needs, business owners and leaders can no longer afford to stay homogeneous in how they operate. Whether you are a CEO running an empire and at the top of your game or someone at the bottom level, and whether your enterprise is privately-owned, a publicly traded company, or simply a nonprofit organization, business today is run differently from how it was a few decades ago. Heck, it is different from how it was run even last year. The world is becoming increasingly more connected, and consumers are becoming better educated.

Whether in your boardroom or breakroom, as a business owner and leader, you can benefit from gaining an understanding of the intricacies of how people from diverse cultures communicate. You can no longer afford to stay in your own bubble and hope your business will continue to thrive. You need to learn how to communicate with people from diverse backgrounds in a more culturally fluent way.

This chapter was inspired by the training I have given over the years to various business owners and leaders. In those sessions, I sought to empower them with fresh perspectives on how to overcome unconscious bias, the benefits of doing business with multicultural communities, and how to attract, retain, and engage a multicultural workforce.

The truth is, when it comes to unconscious bias, we all have it—and some biases are more harmful than others. According to neuroscience experts, if you have a brain, you have bias. Having bias was how our ancestors protected themselves from being eaten by lions and bears. Although the human species has evolved, and lions and bears rarely eat people nowadays, part of our brain is still fearful of the unfamiliar. That fear comes from learned stereotypes deeply rooted in our psyche that often influence our behaviors. We act out of what our parents and caregivers passed down to us when we were growing up. Later, we learned another set of biases from the environment in which we were educated and where we lived. Some of those biases are good because they protect us from unwanted situations. However, some are not so good because they keep us from growing and connecting, and they can unjustly affect those they are directed toward.

These negative biases are what I am writing about—the unconscious biases that prevent people from connecting or crossing cultural boundaries because of the fear of differences, such as race, gender, culture, religion, sexual orientation, disability, socio-economic class, or any other sociological construct.

We have all been in situations where someone said something culturally insensitive that didn't sit well with us. Or we may have said something without even knowing we were offending someone else. How we choose to include or exclude others often says more about us and our level of awareness than it does about those we stereotype.

My hope for this chapter, and the whole book for that matter, is that what I share will cause you to see yourself and others from a different lens and perhaps to stop and say, "I never thought of it that way before!" In other words, I hope to spark your mind with some aha moments and increase your awareness.

If you are a business owner or organizational leader, you are no stranger to taking big risks for big rewards. With those risks also comes a high degree of stress and anxiety that can prevent you from effectively dealing with people you are not familiar with. This is what unconscious bias does to us. It sends messages to our brain to avoid unfamiliar situations or judge people by how different they are from us.

Let us explore an example. An owner of a real estate company once shared a story about one of her female real estate agents. The agent had had an immigrant couple referred to her who wanted to buy a house, so she called the couple to schedule an initial meeting. When she met them, she realized the couple was from an Islamic state. However, she was unfamiliar with Muslims. When she extended her hand to greet them, the wife shook it, but the husband did not.

Imagine you are that agent. What thoughts might rush into your mind at that moment? You may feel that the man was rude and disrespected you by not shaking your hand. While you are assessing the whole situation, you may think, *I'd better get out of here as fast as I can.* You might come up with some excuses, end up not sharing enough information with the prospective home buyers, and run out of there as quickly as possible.

How many of us have misjudged a situation and judged people based on their background or cultural customs because we didn't take the time to understand them? Instead of sitting down to learn why this man didn't shake her hand or learn about the relationship dynamics in the couple's original culture, she ran and possibly left a good sales commission on the table, just because she lacked understanding of their culture. She should have done her homework first and learned about the potential clients' culture. She should have asked questions and not assumed her culture is everyone's culture.

Asking good questions like, "Why don't some Muslim men shake hands with people of the opposite gender?" and "How do people from this culture purchase a home?" would have helped her to understand them better.

The real estate agent could have determined who makes the buying decision in this family (keeping in mind that this family does not represent all Muslim families). Is it the husband, the wife, both, or the in-laws? You might find out that it isn't necessarily the one who makes more money or wears pants in the family. Before you embark on speed-selling or buying, spend some time learning about your potential clients. Learn the dynamics of their gender roles, their generational gaps, and their cultural negotiation tactics.

This knowledge will allow you to connect with your potential customers and build rapport first. While money is important, it cannot buy you relationships. Relationships are built on trust, and trust is earned. When you build trust and have respect for other people's cultures, you will get repeat customers and referrals from multicultural clients.

As a business owner and leader, at some point, you will lead or do business with people who are different from you, or at least have different points of view. That can challenge your beliefs and customs, but it can also stretch and expand your awareness. However, it is entirely up to you. You have the free will to choose whom you do business with, what kind of world you want to live in, and what kind of legacy you want to leave behind.

In my observations, most couples in the American culture decide together, and women play a big part in buying decisions, whether it is a home or an appliance, and in choosing what community to live in. Other cultures, however, might be more patriarchal or matriarchal. If you don't know, don't assume. It is better to ask questions to find out how to interact with people whose culture is different from yours.

I am aware that what I share in this book will not help eliminate unconscious biases. It would be pretentious to think human behaviors are that easy to change. Anything that deals with the human condition cannot be rushed. But I intend to help business owners and leaders become more aware of potential biases so they can make informed decisions in their daily interactions and business dealings.

Diversity and inclusion work is not a one-time event. It must be an ongoing effort that is prioritized by business owners, organizational leaders, and individuals in training and other personal and professional development events. It must be invested in through consistent actions and expanded into the overall organizational culture. To say a community or organization is diverse and inclusive, there has to be an inclusive environment conducive to diversity of thought and experience from people with diverse abilities and identity backgrounds—both of which can be seen and unseen.

Whether you are a business owner or a company executive, the fact that you are reading about diversity and inclusion is already a great step in the right direction. I congratulate you and thank you for making this book a resource for your diversity education efforts.

If you do business in today's world, you need to gain diverse perspectives in solving problems, in both your personal and professional lives. You need to learn how other cultures perceive good customer service and how they perceive time and overtime. You can't do business with people who value building connections if your business practices are like speed dating!

You may be thinking: *But how can I learn about all the cultures? There are way too many out there.* You are right. Of course, you cannot learn everything about every culture. It is impossible. But there is one culture you need to understand better than any other: your own culture —the one wired into your own mindset. Here is why.

Understanding your own culture allows you to know when it hinders your ability to connect with others. It helps you become more tolerant of other people's differences. It also allows you to share what you know with those who are new to your culture; then you become open to learning from your diverse customers, clients, employees, and other stakeholders. In addition, connecting with others requires you to be brave enough to face the often delicate and nuanced uncomfortable feelings when dealing with people from different cultures.

I will be the first to acknowledge that I don't know everything about different cultures or identities. And I have messed up many times by assuming I knew when I didn't. Learning to say, "I am sorry," when you mess up, and doing your best next time, is cultural humility, and that is a leadership trait no one can teach you. It means you acknowledge that you don't know what you don't know, and you are willing to learn as you go.

Begin with yourself; be secure in who you are and who you want to be in the world. Be comfortable learning about uncomfortable topics. As I shared in previous chapters, race is an uncomfortable topic for many people. Learn what you can do as a business leader to lessen the racial equity gap. Becoming familiar with issues that affect some communities in the marketplace and knowing how to interact with those affected can help grow your business. This knowledge shows how much you care about those negatively affected by things you may take for granted.

Like I said before, true privilege is being able to do something about an issue that doesn't affect you personally. Being a successful business owner and leader has to do with looking inside yourself, discovering your values, and knowing what you stand for. Look at your blind spots, your biases—both conscious and unconscious—and decide to use your personal and business power for the greater good.

Don't assume anything by judging people based on the group they belong to. Ask questions instead. Be curious and learn their individual behaviors. It is not helpful to label people as good or bad, because good and bad coexist in all of us. What differentiates people is whether they are aware or unaware, and conscious or unconscious mindsets. And since we are continually evolving in one way or another, it comes down to what side we want to reinforce: the good side or the bad side?

## Honoring Intersecting Identities

A student at the university where I was presenting asked me an important question about intersecting identities. He asked, "I was born in the US, but my parents are Mexicans who came from Mexico. I often feel confused about my national identity when people ask me about my origins. I am not sure if I should say I am Mexican or American, or Mexican American, or just Latino American. What do you think?"

Many young people feel the same confusion when it comes to their cultural identities. My own kids have asked me the same question: "Mom, are we Africans or African Americans?" I must admit, at first, I didn't know what to tell my children. Then it occurred to me that I didn't have to choose one cultural identity over the others.

Cultural diversity is about honoring our intersecting identities and our experiences. I am African, a woman, black, an immigrant, a mother, an author, and an advocate. I am a Christian, and I am straight. I speak three different languages, and my native country's colonial influences from Germany and Belgium are yet another layer of my cultural inheritance. My ethnic background enriches my identity, and I belong to a blend of diverse cultures and subcultures.

We cannot put people in boxes just by looking at them. We need to approach people as individuals and not label them based on groups. We are layers and layers of human complexity, so we should embrace all our identities because we are so much more than our social constructs.

Sometimes people have challenged my diversity and inclusion views by asking me, "So, do you think we should all hug? Is it really possible to love everyone?" To which I reply, "Gosh, no, I'm not that naïve!" Of course, we can't love everybody. We still have in-laws… to love from a distance, you know. But I still think diversity and inclusion are how we come together, make sense of who we are in all our intersecting identities, and use the intersectionality of our privileges to empower one another from a deeper understanding.

While we acknowledge that we are different, at the same time, we find what we have in common. Our commonalities come from the fact that we all want to be accepted for who we are. That is what can unite us in our differences—the need to be seen and validated in our God-given gifts. I may celebrate my uniqueness, but I also enjoy what I have in common with others. We may be different in how we look, speak, or pray, but our common lot is that we all have a human spirit that longs for connection and for the chance to better our lives and the lives of our families. Whether you are a business professional whose job is to close sales or a farmer growing food for a living, that human drive for connection and betterment is similar. Everyone you meet is here for a reason, just like you are. No one is a random creature who happened to populate planet Earth. We were created with a purpose and for a purpose.

Next time you encounter a client who doesn't look like you or is different in any way, don't discredit them just because they are different. Instead, be curious; be interested in their story. We all have a story. If you meet an immigrant, create a rapport by asking them what their journey to America has been like. What are their dreams and hopes? Ask them what it is like buying or selling in their culture. That way, selling to them will be easier for you, and also for them to buy from you, because you connected first and built trust with them. Developing cultural awareness will help you not only grow your business but also foster a culture of inclusion in your organization and your community. It is not just the right thing to do; it is the human thing to do. While you can't learn about every culture, you can practice observing and being curious.

If your business is missing out on opportunities to close sales or get referrals, perhaps your salesforce is only comfortable doing business with people like them. It may be time for you to start investing in employee training to equip them with cultural competency and cross-cultural communication skills.

If diversity and inclusion are important to you and your business—especially if it offers a tremendous benefit to increase your revenues, then get better at it. Hire a coach or a trainer, or simply get mentored in diversity leadership. There is always someone smarter and wiser who can teach us from their perspective. As demographic shifts and trends continue to reflect a change in where and how individuals and communities live, business owners and leaders need to be ready for times of change and build inclusive and welcoming workplaces and communities.

Business leaders can take many steps to foster diversity. The first and most important step is to hire from a diverse pool of qualified candidates. Learn where you can recruit multicultural candidates and invite them to apply for jobs at your company. The second step is getting buy-in from top leadership. You and your senior leaders should make diversity and inclusion an integral part of your business practices, from attracting and hiring talent to employee retention and engagement. Hiring a diverse workforce offers a competitive advantage that can shift market share in your favor.

Below are some of the benefits of having a multicultural workforce.

## 1. Innovation, Creativity, and Revenue

Diverse teams bring diverse solutions and methods to solve often complex organizational challenges. In addition, an inclusive workforce culture ensures you have people who can speak different languages, understand different cultures, better communicate with customers or clients who speak those languages, and bring in new business from other countries and cultures. In return, you will achieve a higher level of income and greater influence by expanding into new territories and markets.

## 2. Social Branding and Responsibility

Diversity and inclusion within your workforce will help your business or organization's social responsibility branding and leadership legacy. Inclusive cultures increase brand awareness and build momentum to attract diverse partners. Having a diverse workforce increases your revenue potential by strengthening existing relationships and forging new ones. It is a winning formula.

### 3. Compliance with Labor and Other Laws

In November 2019, *Newsday* published a story based on an undercover investigation into discrimination by real estate agents on Long Island in New York. "*Newsday* found evidence of widespread separate and unequal treatment of minority potential homebuyers and minority communities on Long Island." [12]

This case caused the real estate industry to think of ways to remedy these Fair Housing and Equal Opportunity Act violations. One suggestion from the real estate industry was to implement fewer disciplinary measures and enhance diversity training for real estate professionals. They realized that to reduce fair housing infractions, it is important for the real estate salesforce to be culturally fluent. Therefore, hiring diverse employees helps reduce legal expenses due to anti-discrimination labor and consumer laws. In addition to avoiding compliance issues, how consumers perceive your company can affect your business' ability to grow. Organizations known for discriminating against their employees or customers will be negatively perceived, while those that embrace diversity, equity, and inclusion may be favorably perceived and earn increased customer loyalty.

## Selling to Multicultural Communities

As a business owner, having a diverse workforce fluent in cultural competency will help attract new clients and customers from multicultural communities, which could potentially make you a lot of money.

According to "*Diversity Matters*," an article by McKinsey and Company, "More diverse companies are believed to be better able to win top talent and improve their customer orientation, employee satisfaction, and decision making, and all that leads to a virtuous cycle of increasing returns." [13]

Let's delve deeper and uncover strategies for effectively selling to diverse multicultural markets. The number one mistake you can make as a business owner or company leader is to assume your mainstream business culture is everybody's business culture. When it comes to minority buyers, even those from the same cultural backgrounds have subcultures, and the way they buy will differ from one ethnic group to another. This means it is not wise to put every ethnic minority in the same box.

For instance, when you hear people say "Asians," "Hispanics," "Africans," "Europeans," "Middle-Easterners," etc., you have to understand that within those cultures are subcultures and differences in how people buy products and services. "Africa" is a common word used to describe African countries, but on the African continent, there are many countries, all with different cultures. For example, West Africa's culture is very different from East Africa's culture in how people behave and operate businesses.

And even within West or East African cultures, there are subcultures based on their history and socio-economic advancement. Things like how buying decisions are made may vary depending on cultural gender roles, generational gaps, bargaining customs, relationship building, and other cultural habits you will need to learn, depending on your potential customers.

Let's look at the business of advertising. While in the United States, certain animals may be used in advertisements because they are perceived as cute, in some cultures, those same animals may represent the total opposite of cuteness. One example is the owl. I have seen TV commercials for eyeglasses using an owl that talks and wears glasses. In my native culture, an owl is perceived as a bad omen. It foretells the death of someone in the vicinity of where the owl was seen or heard. That is the message you might bring across if you use certain animals without knowing their meaning in other cultures.

Another way to avoid cultural stereotypes and biases is to avoid using the same sales pitch for all cultures without properly understanding each. While all Asians might have some cultural similarities, they also have differences. The same applies to other ethnic communities, such as Africans and African Americans. Not all black people share the same culture. And it is the same for Hispanics or people from the Middle East. Each ethnic group has similarities and differences. Not all white people have the same culture either. Some Europeans may share some common business habits with America's mainstream selling culture, but there may also be differences from country to country.

In the age of the Me Too movement, especially in the United States, things like personal space, hugging or not, touching or not, shaking hands or not, making eye contact or not, or kissing four times on the cheek are all cultural differences I have seen that can cause confusion, just like the example I gave earlier of the Muslim couple, where the man refused to shake hands with a female.

Before you create your list of potential products or services to sell to multicultural communities, do your homework. Once you understand those cultural differences, you will be able to sell to multicultural clients without fear of offending them or feeling offended by them. In addition, resist the tendency to put people in boxes; treat them as individuals, and judge them by their individual behaviors, not the behaviors of their group, country, or political party.

Saying things like, "Young black men are thugs," or other dehumanizing terms is how we reinforce biases and widen, rather than bridge, the gap that separates people and communities. That is how the bias against black and African American people was perpetuated, and reinforced inequity and stereotypes. We have seen so many incidents of police brutality against black people in America, and I believe we can only stop these acts of police violence against people of color if we all come together, acknowledge and address the root causes, and choose leaders who are committed to treating all people equitably. We need to speak the truth in a civil and compassionate way and debunk certain biases.

Another example of bias I have heard many times is when talking about Africa. We need to have the right perspective when it comes to Africa and Africans. While many nations in Africa are poor and struggling to develop, calling them names will not help them develop. This is not to condone the failures on the part of some African leaders, especially when I hear them blame colonizers for the lack of development in their countries.

Instead of acting responsibly, they enrich themselves, create divisions among their people, and cause insecurity and endless civil wars, which are the fundamental causes of their underdevelopment. Yes, there is some truth to the idea that Africa was slow in developing because of colonization and the exploitation of Africa's resources. However, Africa can still rise out of poverty and benefit the world economy in a far greater and more equitable way, but only if its leaders start caring and protecting all their people.

What we say, how we say it, and the intention and actions behind the words we use matter. Every human hopes that tomorrow will be better than yesterday, and we fight to be seen, heard, and accepted for who we are. When we experience stereotypes and biases just because we were born a certain way or into certain circumstances, we become more disconnected. Therefore, if you want to grow your business by selling your products and services to people of minority and multicultural backgrounds, it is up to you as a business owner or leader to learn what you don't know by observing your customers and employees and adjusting to what they value.

Every business owner knows the greatest compliment anyone can pay them is to refer them and their business to other customers. If multicultural communities know you don't just care about selling to them, but you genuinely care about them in the way you connect, you will be surprised by how far they can go to support you and your business. When you know how to engage culturally with diverse and multicultural communities, you will get great referrals, and money cannot buy such an endorsement. And so, nurturing your organization's diversity and inclusion in all its divisions is a sure way to support your business' growth.

## Managing a Multicultural Team

To develop cultural fluency in the workplace, managers and supervisors need to know the cultural differences among their teams. Below are four insights to inspire managers in creating inclusive workplaces.

## 1. Cultural Differences in Communication

People from different cultures respond differently to various situations. As a manager, you have to understand how people report good or bad news. You achieve this by asking different groups questions about how their cultures react to news. This will help you know how to effectively communicate both good and bad feedback.

For instance, in the culture I grew up in, we were taught to respect and not challenge authority, even when the person or group in authority was wrong, and we were right. You may have employees who won't share their views because they are afraid of challenging your authority. Another example of a cultural communication difference is that in some cultures, being outspoken is considered a sign that you are smart and confident, while in others, it's viewed as a lack of respect. You might see an employee who is shy and reserved and assume they lack confidence, when instead, they might just be showing you respect. As a manager or supervisor, it is important to learn how your employees from different cultures communicate their needs and to encourage their full engagement.

## 2. Cultural Differences in Work and Life Values

As a manager, you need to identify the values within your teams, such as work-life balance. Some cultures value work relationships over family and vice versa. You should consider your team's cultural expectations and what is important to them.

## 3. Cultural Differences in Teamwork and Supervision

Some societies may have an egalitarian culture that encourages all to participate. However, if you work with people from authoritarian regimes, where they experienced dictatorship, not participation, you may have to be more proactive in asking for their input. This situation can cause friction between managers and employees of diverse cultures. The same is true if you come from a hierarchical, dictatorial culture and manage people in an egalitarian culture. Moreover, in some cultures, like the United States, people were trained from an early age to "do it yourself." Other cultures, however, value cooperation within or among other teams. You will need to adjust your leadership style to strike a balance.

## 4. Cultural Differences in Time Management

Different perceptions of time can cause misunderstandings and turmoil in the workplace, especially concerning scheduling and deadlines. Perception of time is an important aspect of cultural diversity in the workplace, and it can affect production/service goals if not addressed early in the conversation. It needs to be on the menu of every diversity training or seminar.

Cultures differ in how they view time management. In some cultures, time is "elastic" and may not necessarily be the strict number of hours needed to finish a task, as long as the task gets completed. I used to hear people say, "It will get done," and I would think, "But when?" It can be frustrating waiting on someone you know is capable of finishing the job quickly, but who doesn't perceive time the same way you do. As a manager or supervisor, you have to communicate your expectations.

I remember how I used to struggle with deadlines when I first immigrated to North America, but now I have come to love deadlines! I like being on time and look down on tardiness. In the workplace, such differences may influence the perception of break time, overtime, and the exact meaning of a deadline. And these cultural differences exist even between companies. For example, in some European countries like Italy or Spain, it is normal to take two or more hours for lunch breaks. But if you are from the United States, that probably seems extreme. Some cultures may value the quality of life over productivity. You just have to learn how to strike a balance if you are going to do business with people from those cultures.

Now, as a business leader, you may think diversity and inclusion are a nice-to-have only when the economy is doing well, or even think of it as charity for your employees of diverse backgrounds. If that is the case, then you are going about this wrong. As an organizational leader or business owner, understanding how to treat the people you lead or do business with is a cost-saving strategy. Why? Because you won't need to spend so much money trying to promote your business to multicultural communities or get your diverse teams engaged and motivated. If your employees feel you sincerely care about them, they will be your best business promoters.

# CHAPTER 12

# Belonging and Workplace Culture

### Can employees truly bring their whole selves to work?

How much is *TMI—too much information—* to share at work? When I started working in a corporate environment, I was always happy when someone at work asked me if I had children. I eagerly shared how many I had and their ages. However, I also began to fear that the information I shared might be used against me. Unfortunately, in some cases, it was. And so, I found myself in a challenging situation where I had to balance sharing my personal life with maintaining privacy in professional settings.

It felt like I was being asked to wear a mask, leaving my role as a mother behind when I went to work and pretending to be free of family responsibilities. I also noticed that mothers who successfully maintained a separation between their family and work lives were more likely to be taken seriously at work. These mothers had better chances of being promoted or receiving high-profile assignments. This observation made me realize how family responsibilities are often seen as obstacles for mothers who aspire to advance in their careers.

## Should employees mask who they are?

We live in a digitalized world, where getting and sharing personal information is at our fingertips. But when in the workplace, how much is too much information to share with co-workers and leaders? Is it possible for an employee to bring their whole self to work without sharing everything about their personal lives? Another thing is, should employees only share what's good and keep the bad news to themselves? These and more questions are my inquiry when it comes to leadership and authenticity.

I remember a time a friend called me in panic and said, "I cried at work." And I said, "You did?"

Is it ever okay to cry at work? It seems like employees are often given mixed messages. On the one hand, employees are told they can bring their whole selves to work, and on the other hand, they are told not to talk about their personal lives. Furthermore, employees are told not to let their personal lives affect their jobs.

## Authenticity builds connections, but proceed with caution.

The power of sharing personal information lies in its potential to create deeper connections. Authenticity cannot exist without compassion and empathy, which are essential to a connected life. Compassion should be for self and then extend it to others because, without self-compassion, you don't have it to give to others. Empathy is feeling others' emotions, both during their good and challenging seasons of life.

Leaders should remember that employees are more than just contributors—they are unique individuals with their personalities, lived experiences, and perspectives. While discussing topics such as hobbies, interests, or light-hearted conversations can enhance team bonding, it's also important to approach the sharing of more sensitive information, like medical matters or deeply personal details, with caution. Why? Some disclosures may create discomfort for colleagues who may not be equipped to properly respond.

One employee shared that during a performance review meeting, her manager told her that her job performance was very good, but the only problem was that her colleagues had complained about her not sharing her personal life with them. She had to talk to Human Resources and explain that not sharing her personal details with co-workers was her cultural upbringing, which was different from that of her colleagues. In addition, she didn't feel that oversharing personal details with her coworkers was a requirement for performing her job.

This was a case where a manager lacked cultural diversity and imposed that employees share personal details as part of their job performance, even if they didn't feel comfortable. There is a fine line between being friendly with your employees and coworkers, but you can't impose personal sharing as a job requirement.

Therefore, balancing openness with discretion can help maintain a comfortable atmosphere for everyone involved. If you don't know your colleagues very well, they may be dealing with their issues. Things like mental health have gained awareness in the workplace, but are still taboo subjects, depending on one's culture. Some individuals still find these topics uncomfortable, particularly when they relate to workplace environments where employees experience toxicity.

## Authentic leadership is different from managing

Often, leaders confuse the act of leading with managing employees. And so, when it comes to sharing personal information beyond the surface level, it can be challenging for leaders to encourage authenticity if it's not directly conducive to a tangible result. This can be especially challenging if leaders themselves are going through their own issues, such as the stress from upper management to increase performance, such as sales numbers.

Sometimes, it's not possible to separate personal issues from professional ones. Instead of punishing employees for missing the sales quotas, leaders can encourage employees to take time off to heal and seek psychological and emotional support to weather the storms of their personal lives and heal whatever problems are preventing them from fulfilling their responsibilities at work.

## When authenticity meets different cultures

In 2024, I visited France and explored several cities. During my trip, I met up with a friend who lives in Blois, central France, and taught English at a high school in Orléans. One day, my friend invited me to speak to her students about my work in diversity, equity, and inclusion (DEI) in the United States.

In one of my discussions with students about cultural differences, we talked about the differences between French people and Americans. Some students mentioned that they believe Americans are generally more open. My French friend remarked, "Americans often try to make friends quickly, even before getting to know someone well." I then asked, "What about the French?"

One of the students replied, "The French prefer to take their time to get to know a person before considering them a friend."

This is not to say that one culture is better than the other—it is important to recognize that no culture is superior to another. Instead, we must celebrate the diversity of cultures and understand the significant impact they have on individuals, workplaces, and communities.

In some cultures, authenticity means different things to different people. What might come across as too *rowdy* in some cultures can be viewed as a typical American way of freedom of expression. Additionally, in many cultures, asking personal questions is deemed inappropriate unless a strong sense of trust has been established.

For example, simple inquiries like *"How are you?"* are not just casual phrases—they are invitations to delve into someone else's personal life and may be met with skepticism or perceived as insincere in more reserved cultures, where it takes time to build relationships and establish trust.

## Authenticity and discretion

While it is all right to share personal information, it is wise to choose with whom we share those details because not everyone can keep it confidential. And once you share something with someone, there isn't much you can do to control how the information will be used. Unfortunately, some workplaces also experience a culture of negative gossip that can hinder the overall employee experience. This environment creates distrust, affects collaboration, and makes it difficult for employees to feel comfortable bringing their whole selves to work. This is why choosing your circle of trust is important when you need to share personal information. There has to be a delicate balance between being open and being reserved.

## Creating an inclusive workplace culture

While working for a company affiliated with Germany, a German colleague visited our US team from Germany. During lunch, he asked, "Why do Americans ask personal questions?" I replied, "What kind of questions?"

He explained that someone had inquired about which church he attended and that he felt this was intrusive. While the German colleague perceived the question as intrusive, the American asking it may have intended it as a way to connect. However, he should have considered the nuances of German culture first. What might seem like a casual question in America could be viewed as quite personal in Germany. He then made an interesting observation: "With so many churches in America, are Americans really that religious?"

## Creating psychological safety

What can leaders do to encourage authenticity? By creating psychological safety. As a leader, one of the ways you can create psychological safety is by giving grace to people to make mistakes, especially those who might not have the same lived experiences as you. In my case, when presenting, for example, I start by sharing with my audience a moment when I messed up.

Like in the instance I shared in Chapter 11, where I asked a black woman wearing a hijab if she was a Somali, and she said she was born and raised in Dallas, Texas. This example gave my audience the psychological safety of knowing that we all have unconscious biases, and we all mess up sometimes. I wanted my audience to know that DEI is not about knowing everything there is to know. It is about learning what we don't know as we go and do better next time.

That example put them at ease, and they could be vulnerable and share their own moments when they unconsciously said something to someone without realizing it was offensive. It made more people in the audience open up and not feel like they would be shamed if they unintentionally did or said something to someone. I also helped them reflect on what to do when unconscious bias acts up, because it will.

Building psychological safety is also a way of building trust. By sharing my DEI story and building rapport to earn my audience's trust, they felt psychologically safe to share their own mess-up moments, especially when it was about personal vulnerabilities. I don't force people to open up; I just create an environment where those who are ready can feel psychologically safe to share their unconscious moments. The following are some of the ways leaders can encourage employees to bring their authentic selves to work in a manner that respects their individuality, while being inclusive.

- Asking questions to learn about authenticity with a nuanced approach according to employees' cultural heritage.
- Giving employees a safe space to be authentic to themselves without feeling compelled to overshare.
- Engaging with employees' work with integrity and not at the expense of their personal privacy and mental well-being.
- Encouraging employees to explore others' sense of authenticity so they can work together with teams in harmony.

Leaders need to recognize and respect that different cultures may approach this differently, and this is where the beauty of cultural diversity lies. By understanding this, organizational leaders and employees can work together to navigate workplace authenticity and respect individual cultural values while enhancing the overall inclusive environment.

In the end, creating an inclusive workplace culture that fosters belonging means encouraging employees to show up as their best selves in a professional, respectful, and engaged manner.

It is when a leader encourages their employee and says, "You can do this assignment, I believe in you." To the employee, that translates into *I see you, you matter, and you belong here.*

It is equally important to maintain healthy boundaries between one's personal and professional life. This balance promotes trust and builds a workplace environment where everyone can thrive.

# CHAPTER 13

# Working as a DEI Practitioner

Working as a diversity, equity, and inclusion advocate has allowed me to learn from and teach diverse people in diverse settings. One thing I have learned in this field is that diversity leadership is not for the faint of heart. It is a relatively new profession, and for me, it has been mostly exciting but also challenging. But above all, it has been rewarding.

In this chapter, I thought I would share some dos and don'ts for diversity, equity, and inclusion practitioners. By no means do I claim to have an exhaustive list of answers to all diversity questions or nuances. These are observations mostly based on my experiences, both personally and professionally. Go ahead and add your dos and don'ts, whether you are a leader trying to build an inclusive culture in your organization or a diversity practitioner helping leaders with diversity best practices.

The journey to becoming a diversity leader might be easy for some, but for many, it will be a bumpy ride. As you embark on or continue your diversity leadership journey, you may have to deal with some of those bumps in the road. Below, let's explore the ways you can deal with some of them and promote an inclusive culture in your workplace and community.

## A. Dealing with Skepticism

During your diversity work, you will encounter people who, no matter what you do or don't do, and no matter how you do it, will not be enthusiastic about what you are trying to create. For some people, just hearing the word *diversity* ignites a fight-or-flight response. It's difficult to teach new perspectives to people with this mindset because they have already adopted a blockage mentality. No matter what you say to them, it will not penetrate their minds. They will use all types of tactics, from belittling your message and criticizing and judging you to saying things that are simply not true or proven. They might say things like:

- "We don't need inclusion. I've worked hard for what I have."
- "I live on the same street and in the same neighborhood as black and brown people. How am I more privileged than they are?"
- "There is nothing new in this diversity and inclusion talk—nothing I haven't heard before."
- "Why are black people still complaining about discrimination? Slavery was over more than 100 years ago. It's just an excuse to be lazy."

I cringed when I heard someone say that last one in a community-based setting.

Here is another example I found on social media. Following an article about how one executive was implementing diversity and inclusion in his company, one person commented:

> *People are stuck on color and gender like it's the '60s, and they're proud of it. They count the number of this or that,*

*then pat themselves on the back. It's racist and sexist to hire or promote based upon those criteria, but they do it and feel great about it.*

As a diversity practitioner in your organization, how can you respond to skeptics like these? As you can see in the example above, not everyone will get on board or be there to help you build an inclusive environment, and some of the resistance may actually have some validity. You can't just dismiss every skeptic as being "racist" or "an insensitive person." It will be your job to get the skeptics to believe in your diversity vision by showing them that more inclusion means more potential for increased business success, where everyone can benefit.

Becoming an inclusive leader is a balancing act, which means you need to promote women and minorities in order to build a balanced leadership team in your organization. Promoting gender diversity among top management is beneficial for the company because women make more buying decisions than men, and it is proof that your company is socially responsible, which is becoming more and more important to consumers.

Advocating for gender pay equality doesn't mean women are asking to take away men's salaries. They just want equal pay for equal work between men and women. If done correctly, the inclusion of others should not feel like the exclusion of some. This is how it has been so far, and that is why, as diversity practitioners, we are working to reverse the situation of inequities and exclusions. But, of course, some people have a sense of entitlement and don't think we need to advocate for equity and inclusion because they have never experienced what it is like to be excluded. Some will let you know their thoughts, and some will not. But, as shown in the example above, they might think this whole diversity work is simply "reverse racism."

What can you do to make sure more people in your organization buy into your ideas of inclusion? Today, artificial intelligence software is being used to help take bias out of the hiring process. However useful technology may be in the hiring process, it is not going to do your diversity work. You must appeal to people's diverse experiences and meet them where they are. For example, are employees satisfied with their working conditions? How about their personal lives? Find where people are and how you, as a diversity and inclusion leader, can help alleviate their pain. Remember, this is a human issue; it's not just about money or things. While this method might not get every skeptic to agree with your ideas, some will come around. First, work with just the few who come around, and gradually expand your circle of diversity, equity, and inclusion supporters.

When you meet resistance or skepticism in your diversity and inclusion efforts, humble yourself in the knowledge that you are among flawed humans, and each person is responsible for their own personal growth. Don't expect everyone to increase their awareness at the same speed or depth as everyone else. Take a deep breath and ask yourself, "Why is this person resistant to my ideas? What is it they are going through?" Once you know the root causes of their resistance, then you can address them to the best of your abilities.

As you evolve your consciousness, you also need to acknowledge that the journey may take longer for some people. But don't let the skeptics discourage you from your mission. You cannot change other people's behaviors, and humans only change when they feel they have to. Some will do, but alas, some may never make that choice. At the end of the day, this work is about opening people's minds, not changing their behaviors. You can't change anyone without their consent. What you can do when you meet resistance is stop and listen, then reflect on the validity of those opposing views. You may find something enriching for your growth and even some inspiration for your diversity leadership. Listening to the naysayers and skeptics can bring people together and help them find a common goal to connect over, thus improving inclusivity. It might help to clarify that including the historically marginalized, underserved, and underrepresented is not about excluding those who are privileged by their socio-economic backgrounds. More inclusion should be more, not less.

If not careful, others' skepticism could cause you, as a diversity, equity, and inclusion proponent, to lose track of your mission and get discouraged. You may even end up alienating people instead of working for a common purpose. Always remember that being an inclusive leader begins within. Shift your mindset toward inclusivity and gain new perspectives to expand your own awareness of the diversity within and around you. That way, you will be able to partner with people who support you and bring in new diversity allies by creating a welcoming environment for all. People support what they help create.

Also helpful is learning about other people's unique and diverse identities. We cannot create inclusive cultures if we are alienating those who don't share our identities. For instance, even though I am an advocate for multicultural diversity based on my race, culture, and gender, there are other minorities and people whose identity backgrounds I don't share, so I need to learn about them and include them in my diversity, equity, and inclusion mission. I need to learn about their challenges and opportunities, so I don't put people in a box.

Below are some strategies for getting buy-in from diverse stakeholders if you want to build an inclusive culture in your organization. Please know this is not an exhaustive list by any stretch of the imagination. But it will get you started, and you can think of more ideas as you go.

## How to get diversity and inclusion buy-in?

1. Choose a few supporters from different departments, business units, and teams. Get buy-in from the top to the bottom of your organizational leadership.
2. Open brave spaces for conversations to allow exchanges of experiences from others. The term "brave space" was developed by some scholars, mainly to complement the term "safe space." It was first made popular by Brian Arao and Kristi Clemens in their book *The Art of Effective Facilitation* in a chapter titled "From Safe Spaces to Brave Spaces." [14]

    The way I understand "brave space" versus "safe space" is that, in addition to being safe to say what you feel without repercussions as in a safe space, you also discuss your thoughts and feelings with the group, engaging in conversations on difficult topics such as human differences, and holding each person accountable for doing the work of sharing their experiences and coming to a new understanding.

    We want a "brave space" because some concepts might provoke emotional discomfort, requiring us to be brave enough to broach the difficult subjects. It is not realistic to just have a safe space to express your own feelings when exploring issues that might provoke negative emotions in others. Some of the concepts I write about in this book may rattle some cages and provoke different kinds of emotions and responses, but they come from a brave space and are open to discussion.

The concepts of race and privilege, for example, may make some people feel uncomfortable. However, we cannot continue hiding these issues under the rug, hoping they will just go away if we ignore them. Therefore, having brave spaces ensures we can have a dialogue despite the triggered emotions. Brave spaces also provide people who experience uncomfortable feelings about difficult topics with the opportunity to reflect on why they are uncomfortable. By the same token, they can be responsible and accountable for their emotions and choose how to respond depending on their unique needs.

3. Listen to the skeptics; be interested in their perspectives. Ask them what they want the world to be like when their kids are adults in the workplace.
4. Find common goals by reaching out to build relationships and allyships. Ask the skeptics what they are most passionate about and how you can collaborate with them on what they want to build, considering it's something that can improve the world or the workplace.
5. Ask yourself, "What is my end goal? What do I want to achieve, and what will it look like when I'm done?" This is about having a clear mission of what you want to build,

and it starts in your mind, but you will need to share it with others and get input from them to help you carry it out. What legacy do you want to leave long after you have left the company or the earth?
6. Show that being more inclusive is being business savvy and means more, not less.
7. Connect with the skeptics on a personal level. Invite them to meet you, perhaps have coffee and chat. Get to know them. What is their work-life situation? Ask about their family situation; specific details are not necessary, but only inquire about what they are comfortable sharing, particularly if it relates to fulfilling their work. This conversation is so you can meet them where they are in their current situation. You never know what you might unlock when you take an interest in other people's lives and connect with them on a human level.

   Some people are hurting in their personal lives, so the last thing they want to do is support any cause, and that has nothing to do with you. Even if they end up not supporting you, at least you will have made them feel like they matter. Isn't that what the diversity profession should be about—making people feel like they belong and matter?
8. Don't shame people or make them feel guilty because of their privilege. It is okay to share your personal experiences and how they have made you more resilient and shaped your beliefs. But don't shame people by coming off as too spiteful or resentful about things from the past. That is a sure way to create more skepticism and chase away prospective allies.

9. Acknowledge your limitations and your own privilege. We all have privileges. Share moments when you were uncomfortable with an idea or a situation, or when you were unwilling to change. Share how you overcame your skepticism about an issue, and the outcome—how you changed and what you learned about yourself and others. For example, as a newcomer to North America, I hated it when people made stereotypical comments about Africa or Africans. It made me bitter, and I started hiding where I came from whenever people asked me. I wanted to fit in and belong. But then I realized those people were acting out of their unconscious mindsets, and it was my choice to be bitter or better. That is when I began to work on my understanding of differences and educate myself about diversity and inclusion in our communities and workplaces.
10. Use stories to illustrate what you want people to learn.
11. Answer people's questions and invite them to share their stories and experiences. We all have a diversity story, and every story matters because who we are matters.
12. Above all, be teachable, be curious, and be resilient. As the expression goes: *Let your stumbles make you humble.* Understand that you are not an expert on everything. All great teachers are the best students; it is better to ask questions than make assumptions.

## B. Diversity and inclusion practitioners' pitfalls

As you continue this work of diversity and inclusion and learn to mitigate the skepticism, you also need to be aware of the pitfalls you might experience as a diversity proponent in your organization. To make a real contribution to the diversity mission, you need to leave the diversity policy binder on the shelf and practice real inclusion.

I have seen organizations so proud of how wonderful they were in their diversity and inclusion work, showing off diversity websites that flashed with images of diverse people downloaded from the public domain. But when I took a deep look inside the organization, especially upper management, I only saw one or two minorities or women. The rest of the team? Well, not so diverse. And that is okay if that is the kind of organization you want. However, do not kid yourself and others by claiming your organization is invested in diversity when all you have is a diversity binder and a website.

While some of the roadblocks will come from those who don't think diversity, equity, and inclusion matter, others may come as a shock. They may be from those you are trying to help—those who stand to benefit the most from your efforts. I have been involved with some people whom I thought were for me, but who ended up being roadblocks to what I was trying to achieve because I wanted everyone to feel like they belonged. I have also been denied opportunities by the very people who claimed they were working for diversity, equity, and inclusion because they saw me as the competition, instead of an ally. I understand this reaction comes from feeling that there isn't enough to go around for everyone; it's a scarcity mentality.

Also, resist the temptation to compare ethnic groups based on stereotypes. For example, Asians versus African Americans or Hispanics, etc., resulting in people from one group or another being overly favored over the others in getting hired or promoted.

In addition to comparing and competing, another pitfall for diversity practitioners comes from acting on your own behalf or on behalf of those of your own kind. These may be people of your race, gender, sexual identity, religion, nationality, political ideology, or ethnic background.

If you are promoting diversity acceptance for your group only and discounting other minority groups' experiences, that is not inclusion work. Creating inclusive cultures is not about just advocating for your people. As a diversity and inclusion advocate, you must advocate for everyone in the areas where there are equity gaps. If you are advocating for including more Asians in the movie or entertainment industry, you should also advocate for other underrepresented minorities in that industry. The same applies if you are advocating for the African American, Hispanic, or Native American communities, or any other ethnic group. Always make sure your work benefits all groups, not just your own. As I keep saying, more inclusion should mean more, not less.

Remember that our world is already beautiful. We are standing on the shoulders of giants like Mahatma Gandhi, Martin Luther King Jr., Nelson Mandela, Harriett Tubman, Kwame Nkrumah (who led the Republic of Ghana to become the first sub-Saharan African country to gain its independence from European colonization in 1957), and many others who have weathered battles before us to make our world better. As much as our world is not perfect, we know it is a much better world today than it was a few centuries ago, or even a few decades ago, when slavery, colonization, South African Apartheid, and American Jim Crow segregation laws still ruled.

We have come a long way, and that is why this work of diversity, equity, and inclusion is so important. We don't want to go back to ancient practices and beliefs that no longer have a place in our society. And we want to dismantle systemic injustices that are still affecting some demographics.

It is only right that we express our gratitude not only for those who came before us and fought our battles, but also for those in the fight for equity and inclusion today. Let us thank those who are working to make our workplaces and communities inclusive. The next time you see an employee, manager, or CEO who you know is involved in diversity and inclusion work, take time to thank them.

Knowing others are noticing their efforts will put a spring in their step. We all have a universal yearning to feel validated and know that what we do matters.

## C. The good news

When you go back and read about the awareness stages I shared in the introduction of this book, you may think, "I am nowhere near that conscious mindset, so I can't do much work for diversity." You know what? You are in good company! We are all works in progress; no one is ever completely there, and that is good news. Why? Because if you want to change, you can. It is a matter of free will. Mindsets are not set in stone; they evolve. That is why the second stage in our consciousness is the *evolving mindset*. It is a good mindset to operate from because you keep working on improving yourself and moving into a conscious mindset.

Also, as a diversity practitioner, one question I get from those on the inclusion journey is: "What if my mindset is evolving, but the people around me are not willing to change?" That is a great question to ask. As I wrote in the first section of this chapter, when

I talked about dealing with skepticism, I know that you don't need to judge anyone else. Remember, the only person you need to work on and change is you. You can't change or control other people's behaviors, no matter who you are. Darn, I know! But you can inspire others with your behaviors. It is up to you to choose to evolve your mindset, and as you do so, know that people cope differently with life's challenges and will evolve at different times.

Start now, and remember it doesn't matter when you get there, as long as you begin your evolution today. Refrain from judging late bloomers in this diversity and inclusion work. We all come from different life experiences that prompt us to act in certain ways. That is why this book is about unlocking diversity—to help unlock pre-existing ideas and awaken to our potential to expand how we live, learn, and lead in a world of differences.

I started advocating for diversity as a refugee, then an immigrant trying to integrate into my new culture, and the road to that integration has not been a smooth one. It was paved with challenges and disappointments. But I persisted because I knew the work was bigger than just my ego. On the one hand, it provided insights to those without the same experiences as most refugees or immigrants, and on the other hand, it provided advocacy for those from underserved communities.

As I persisted in this diversity and inclusion work, I encountered people from diverse walks of life, and I realized many were acting out of an unconscious mindset. They had not been exposed to people from different racial or cultural backgrounds. Their biases stemmed from a lack of awareness and an implicit fear of differences. They might not be racist, but they made racist statements.

Being an advocate means you are willing to stand up for issues that affect those who are marginalized because of who they are, and especially, because of things they can't change about themselves. My son perfectly illustrated this point for me when he was seven years old. He went to an event where he met a little white boy, maybe five years old. The little boy looked intensely at my son, and after a while, approached and asked him, "Why are you black?" My son replied, "Because that's how God made me." Satisfied with the answer, the little boy returned to his seat beside his mom. No more questions! Kids are so smart, so pure, and so innocent. Imagine if this conversation had taken place between two adults.

My son was right. The way we are is exactly how God made us. It sounds simple, and yet, it is the truth. I wish more parents would teach this basic truth to their children, instead of arguing about it. I truly believe it would reduce bullying among young people and increase acceptance.

The unconscious mindset restricts not only family relationships but also the workplace and community dynamics. Instead of learning what we don't know, we distance ourselves from those affected by discrimination and injustice because we are not affected by it. As a diversity practitioner, first secure your understanding, grow your diversity and inclusion muscles, and then train others on how to grow their muscles. Along the way, expect resistance and skepticism, pain and discomfort.

Most importantly, be patient with yourself and others; cut yourself some slack. Diversity, equity, and inclusion work is about empowering people, and it is not linear. It looks like a stock market chart, with its ups and downs, back and forth, and everything in between. It's just like life with its contrasting moments. Diversity is not just about race or gender, and it is certainly not about just black and white. It looks like a rainbow with diverse identities and ideas. Diversity is about appreciating what makes humans human. It helps us explore our full potential, which comes from our human differences, and to do so in a welcoming environment.

As a diversity professional, you will make mistakes along the way. Learn from them and grow as a person and a leader. Keep evolving your mindset and moving forward. You will realize that change takes time; everything worth changing will take time and work. You might not even get to see the fruits of your labor until much later, or even generations later.

Many of the positive changes we see today were instigated by people who didn't get to see them come to fruition in their lifetimes. Or they might have seen the results much later in their lives.

Therefore, being a diversity worker is not about instant results or gratification, or about just initiating a few events. For instance, the gender pay equality we are still advocating for today might not be fully realized for another generation. That doesn't mean we give up talking about and advocating for it. Changing human behavior takes time, energy, and resources.

Furthermore, you will realize that being a diversity and inclusion practitioner is not about being a perfect leader. It is imperfect work, done by imperfect people, in an imperfect world. As long as you are doing your best, from where you are and with what you know, and doing it with integrity, know that it is enough—you are enough. Keep learning and growing.

## Getting into the DEI arena

When you work on racial, cultural discrimination, and bias issues, you respond to events that not only affect you, but also your local, regional, national, and global community.

As I said before, when I first immigrated to North America, I had a hard time with being different. Sometimes, it was because people made insensitive jokes or asked stereotypical questions. Those stereotypical questions made me feel insecure about my origins. And I know this to be the experience of many refugees, mostly because of the war stigma we carry.

According to the United Nations Refugee Agency (UNHCR), war refugees are those who have moved from their home country to another country, either because of armed conflict and strife or political repression. This classification was based on the 1951 Refugee Convention, which was drafted to protect the more than 60 million people fleeing World War II, and those who couldn't return to their home countries after the war.[12]

I started witnessing civil wars and destruction in my country as a first grader in 1972, where ethnicity (the two major ethnic groups in Burundi being Hutus and Tutsis) played a big role in the war, just as it did in 1988, and the subsequent wars of 1991 and 1993.

In 1993, the war started when I was in Canada, and I couldn't return because it lasted more than ten years. When you have experienced war, that trauma travels with you. It's not a one-time event you can just shake off because you left your country of origin. Imagine being uprooted, through no fault of your own, and everything and everyone you know stays behind; then you have to start over in a new country and a new culture.

While some of the stereotypical questions I received came from people who were either insensitive or unaware of other races, cultures, and experiences, I also encountered many people who asked me real questions because they genuinely wanted to connect with me. They wanted to learn something about places they had never been to or people they had never met. That was when I decided to turn my experiences of feeling excluded into teachable moments.

I realized I couldn't control what other people say or how they behave. But I had the power to choose how to respond. I chose to advocate for diversity and educate others about it. Of course, we are all different, and that is a good thing. But we also have more in common than what divides us. Dividing people is easier than uniting them, and destroying institutions and communities is also easier than building them.

My response to feeling marginalized became that of bridging the gaps between our diverse and multicultural communities, and sharing perspectives that help people relate to one another, no matter their race, gender, sexual orientation, religion, nationality, or any other social identity. And that is how I became a diversity advocate, supporting the creation of inclusive cultures in the workplace, schools, and communities where people live, work, and play.

## The Million-dollar question

As someone who has lived in both Canada and the United States, one of the questions I get asked a lot is: "What is the difference between living in Canada and the United States?" And depending on who is asking the question, some want to know if Canadians are more accepting of diversity than Americans, while others want to know where life is easier—Canada or the United States. Of course, my assessment is from my personal experiences during the time I lived in both countries.

I would say both Canada and the United States are wonderful countries built on the principles of democracy. However, life has its inconsistencies anywhere you live, and how good life is often depends on how you handle its moments. I usually try to disentangle this question in terms of the socio-economic differences between the two countries.

When I immigrated to the United States, it was mainly because I couldn't find good jobs in my field of study. Even though I had two bachelor's degrees, one in history and another in finance, I could only find entry-level jobs that had nothing to do with my fields of study. But Canada has changed a lot since the 1990s, when I lived there. It has welcomed more refugees than any other country in the Western hemisphere. And more immigrants have now found jobs in different sectors of the Canadian economy than when I lived there. And if you want to talk about healthcare access, there are major differences. Canada has universal healthcare, while the United States is still working on defining the model it wants to adopt, which means many Americans have no access to basic healthcare.

As for accepting differences, just like in the United States, in Canada, it depended on the community where you lived. I have experienced living in communities that were welcoming to immigrants, as well as those where people would ask me, "When are you going back to your country?" I wanted to say, "I just got here. What's your excuse? When are you going back to your country?"

Let's keep in mind that if you're not Native American, First Nations, or Aboriginal, we all share a common thread—everyone here has roots that trace back to different corners of the world. We are all immigrants in one way or another, bringing diverse stories and cultures with us. Whether you arrived yesterday or your ancestors came during the early seventeenth century, we share that common history. We all came to America for various reasons that can be expressed in one phrase: the search for a better life. I have also lived in communities where people were very accepting and caring, both in Canada and the United States.

Life is not perfect in either country or anywhere, for that matter. That is the reality of our human experience; some people are going to be more accepting of diversity than others. America has always been that special country that many people looked at as the model of free enterprise, where you can dream of improving your life. Yes, some people have succeeded, but there are real hardships here too; just take a look at the homelessness in our big cities.

Sometimes people come to America naively expecting to live a hardship-free life and are disillusioned. Many immigrants have been partly to blame for not being honest about their lives in America, because they didn't like telling the people they left behind that living in America could be hard.

In many cases, immigrants are the support system for their relatives, and they cannot bear to tell them the truth because they are the lucky ones who got to come to America. The lucky ones who escaped tremendous hardships and strife in their home countries. I have seen many immigrants (me included) use loans so they could afford to visit and support their relatives, even though they could barely afford to feed their own families or pay their debts here in America. We cannot forget that our free enterprise system doesn't mean life is easy in America.

# CHAPTER 14

# Creating a Ripple of Inclusive Cultures

The best thing we can do with our individual and collective privileges is to take time to reflect on them and then choose how we want to use them to benefit humanity. Life is energy; it is a give and take. We give some, and we take some. And we shouldn't take more than we are willing to give, because it creates an imbalance in our resource distribution.

The following section is about equity in the context of diversity leadership. Confusion often exists between equity and equality, so here I want to clarify the difference between these two concepts.

## Equity versus Equality

*Equity*: According to the dictionary, when not referring to the financial term, "equity is the quality of being fair." Notice, the definition says, "equity is the quality." It doesn't say, "equity is equality." Therefore, *equity* is the fairness that comes from an understanding that, since not all people start at the same level, we must take into consideration their individual needs. This means not every person is given the same things, but only what they need on an individual basis. Although I can't analyze each scenario, suffice it to say that equity encompasses socio-economic and judicial systems and programs that consider the unique needs of groups and individuals, and meet those groups and individuals where they are on the pyramid of needs, as I discussed in the introduction, based on Maslow's *Hierarchy of Needs*.

Having equity is treating people with fairness and giving them access to resources and information. For example, veterans who return from duty in Afghanistan have unique needs when it comes to employment opportunities. They need equity programs that consider their unique situation. In this case, the workplace could initiate diversity programs, such as a mental health program to support veterans when they return from active duty. Another example could be providing daycare facilities in the workplace to support working mothers. Basically, equity takes into consideration that diverse people have diverse needs for reaching their full potential. An important part of advancing equity is building systems in your government, organization, or community that promote inclusion and access for all; in addition to having fair and just policies and systems that reinforce equitable practices, for instance, in the criminal justice system.

Thus, creating an inclusive and equitable leadership culture means that when you receive advantages inherent to your privilege, you should also provide advantages from your privilege to those who might be struggling in the areas where you have more freedoms and favors.

Some people may wonder whether equity and equality are interchangeable. According to the United States Declaration of Independence, "All men are created equal, they are endowed by their Creator with certain unalienable Rights, that among these are Life, Liberty, and the pursuit of Happiness."

Although everyone being equal is a cherished part of the American heritage and a wonderful ideal to hold, I would say it is not completely realistic. Yes, of course, all life has equal value; that's not up for debate. But at the same time, while the ideal of equality is a noble purpose, I like the notion of equity better because, in life, people don't start at the same level. Why? On the one hand, having equal opportunity, for example, would mean that every individual has the same opportunities, and we know that is not the case. We don't have the same advantages in life, the same wealth, the same looks, the same family size.

Wouldn't it be nice if everyone had the same things and was successful in the same way? Maybe, or maybe not! On the other hand, it would also mean that we face the same adversity and are equally equipped to cope with and overcome it. But the reality is, we do not face the same adversity, and we do not overcome it in the same way. Therefore, equity is much more achievable.

We live in an age when information is at our fingertips for better or worse. Today, the information is on your phone or recited by you in a nice voice. You don't even have to type anything into the search engine; just say: "Hey, Siri…," or "Alexa…," or "Okay, Google…." or ChatGPT it. These technological advantages got me thinking: Can societies be equal? Just thinking in terms of internet connectivity, what about those places where they don't have a 24/7 internet connection or Wi-Fi? As I write this book, even though technological advances are making it easy for many of us to access information, especially in Western society, there are still places, even in developed countries, where internet connectivity is limited because of economic disadvantages.

I once traveled to a US state in the Midwest to visit relatives who lived in a majority black neighborhood. I needed to print something and went to the neighborhood library. They had three computers and one printer. You had to make a reservation at least two hours ahead to use them. You were only allowed one hour on the computer, and some days, you couldn't get a spot. In addition, the library only had a few old books that were covered with dust. It was then that I realized not everyone in the US enjoyed an abundance of access to books or computers. Later, when I went to pick up my first-grade nephew from school, I noticed the school was surrounded by many police officers.

I thought there had been a school shooting or something, but I was told that's how the school is normally policed. And this was an elementary school. I wondered what seeing so many police officers every day could be doing to these young kids' minds. What about the neighborhood in general? What if, instead of having heavy policing, the city could increase computer and internet access in its library? People could go to school online, work online, apply for jobs online, or simply enjoy other information resources. With a better education, those people could get better jobs and achieve a better standard of living; then, there would be less neighborhood crime, and consequently, less need for policing. In the end, education would be a win-win for the whole community.

To create inclusive cultures, we, as a society, shouldn't spend time debating how to achieve equality, but we should be working on achieving equity, which is giving people what they need, considering where they are in life. Since we don't all start from the same circumstances, have similar backgrounds, or similar interests, instead of spending time and energy figuring out the equality equation, we should focus on increasing equity because equity focuses on eliminating barriers that have prevented underserved or underrepresented groups from full participation in society.

Let's look at some applications of equity for the real world. Note: This is not an exhaustive list, and some of these applications may overlap with one another.

- Equity in the workplace: during the hiring process, paying, retaining, promoting, appraising, and engaging employees equitably.
- Equity in the education system: admitting, retaining, and graduating equitably.
- Equity in the community development: policing, safeguarding, serving, engaging, building, and housing all done equitably.
- Equity in health access: accessing healthcare and being treated and healed equitably.
- Equity in economic development: access, education, employment, development, healthcare, and wealth creation.
- Equity in access to justice: being equitably judged without prejudice.

## Leading with an Inclusive Mindset

Creating inclusive cultures should be treated as an investment in our children and future generations. We must keep at it and improve on it until more inclusion means more and not less.

From an early age, I learned that humanity is interconnected. Listening to the news on my grandpa's radio as a little girl living with my grandparents on my mother's side, I realized that events happening in distant parts of the world could impact us, even in our remote village.

From a diversity and inclusion perspective, when you create more inclusion in your organization or community, you activate a ripple effect of giving and receiving, which creates more inclusion for more people. Maybe you are in a hiring position and could hire a single mother who needs a job to provide for her children. In this way, your privilege not only benefits you, but it can also feed someone else's child. Or you can hire a veteran who is bouncing from job to job without a steady income. It could be a young person who needs that first job to build a resume, or the man or woman who doesn't even get a chance to be called for a job interview because of their foreign name and accent. You could hire a mother returning to work after years of staying home to care for her family, even if her resume shows employment gaps. Or perhaps, you could mentor a high school kid who is being bullied because of their gender identity or national origin.

How about an immigrant who is working two jobs to feed not only their own family, but to provide for the people they left behind in their country of origin? Most immigrants send money to their home countries, and I am a witness to that. According to the World Bank, "An estimated $625 billion (USD) worldwide was sent by migrants to individuals in their home countries in 2017." [15]

Of that amount, $41 billion was sent by immigrants to their home countries in sub-Saharan Africa, according to a PEW Research Center analysis. [16]

You just never know who else your privilege is positively affecting. I hope my reflections provide you with insight into your work as an educator, business owner, corporate leader, community organizer, and whatever other role you hold. Please share with me your feedback and how you have used these reflections in your work, or simply how they have influenced your own life. My contact information is at the end of this book.

We need to show up and learn from each other's stories. If your identity background comes with certain advantages that have given you a head start, please know that some people are struggling because of who they are. Of course, your success might come from hard work, which may be why you enjoy certain privileges. But at the same time, stop and look around you. Is everyone doing equal work with equal skills, enjoying the same advantages? I don't ask so you will feel guilty about your privilege. I just want to spark your mind to acknowledge your privilege and decide whether you want to use it to benefit your fellow humans.

As I have shared throughout this book, my gift has been realizing that even though I have disadvantages in some areas, I have privileges in others, beginning with the gift of the education I received. Like most people, I have privileges in some facets of life. My education has helped me meet people where they are in their journeys. Thus, we need to be kind, compassionate, and empathetic toward others, knowing we have been blessed with something others may not have.

Maybe you are thinking of your privilege, or maybe you don't feel you have any privilege. Since hearing the story of the Jewish gay man whom I talked about in my TEDx talk, "We Are Not All That Different," and what he went through, including being forced by his family to undergo electroshock therapy to try to turn him straight, I started putting things into perspective.

From that day on, I haven't looked at the word privilege quite the same. It would be a great exercise to take an inventory of your privileges, align them with a purpose, and go where your purpose and passion meet the world's needs. Through this acknowledgment of your privileges, you can use your life to build strong and healthy workplaces and communities, raise strong and healthy families, and educate strong and smart students who will make a positive difference in our world with humility and poise.

When it comes to racial wounds, the only way we can heal our society is by giving each other time and space to talk about racial issues and explore our humanity together. Otherwise, if people keep living from the wounded parts of themselves, there will always be divisions. We need to acknowledge the past because we can't change what we don't acknowledge. Then we need to create inclusive cultures, devoid of racial and social injustices, and forgive and move forward. Is it easy? Oh, no! Is it necessary? Yes. Can we do it? You bet!

We know it's possible if we are individually and collectively willing to change systems of inequity. I often say systemic injustices didn't put themselves into place—people did. And so, only people can take them down. If Germany was able to move past two world wars, unify its territories and people after the Berlin Wall fell, and become one of the strongest economies in the world, then we can certainly rebuild our society and do better. Many countries have rebuilt from nothing and are a testimony that when we want to, we can. Each one of us is called to step up, use our privileges, and meet our local and global challenges with an inclusive consciousness.

## Becoming an inclusive champion

### 1. Be mindful of your communication and its effect

Whether you use words or emojis, communication is the most powerful force available to humanity. How you express yourself as a leader, especially when talking about diversity and inclusion, can make or break your business. In this book, I shared several examples of language that can include or exclude. As a leader, you are called to remember that inclusion is not about taking away someone else's privilege, but rather, it is about inviting more of "them" to become a part of "us."

### 2. Reflect

To create anything worthwhile, you must first take time to focus and reflect, and then rectify or change what is not working, and finally reinforce what is working. The same model applies when you want to create inclusive cultures. Most leaders mean well when they say they want diversity and inclusion in their organizations, but then they lack the vision on how to go about it. If this is the case in your company, learn what needs to be done. Bring in new and fresh perspectives from outside the company to help you. Instead of being defensive, be receptive to feedback from those who are affected by your leadership. You need to reflect and ask yourself: *What problem do I need to solve when it comes to inclusion, and what can I change to improve it? Who is affected by my leadership and how?*

### 3. Repurpose

Creating an inclusive culture is not just nice to have, but a necessary business driver that can help your organization thrive with more innovation, creativity, and global appeal, especially in this new era when workplaces are no longer restricted to a physical space but are expanding to working remotely. This transition should be good news for any business owner or organization leader who wants to harness the power of diversity, equity, and inclusion. It means you can expand your business without limits and reach more customers all over the world. In today's evolving digital economy, more than ever before, your organization's success depends on how you treat your people, both in and outside of the office.

I hope this book gives you the inspiration and motivation to create inclusive cultures in your workplace and community, even when it is hard. In conclusion, I have added some reflection questions for you to ponder. I recommend using a journal to have more space to write.

In today's global economy, we cannot afford to continue to live unconsciously. The world is more interconnected and interdependent than ever before, and therefore, it calls for inclusive leadership. We need to leave behind the politics of division and extremism and come back to the center to find a common purpose, which is creating inclusive cultures where everyone can thrive. We cannot wait idly by and hope that someone else is working on achieving equity and inclusion; it's a call we can all answer, each in our capacity.

Remember, your diversity, equity, and inclusion journey is not a one-time event or something you do only when the economy is good. It's a daily practice that takes conscious effort to learn, teach, and invest in.

I can't wait to hear from you about the results of your efforts in creating an inclusive culture in your organization and community.

If there is anything I can do to help you make your diversity and inclusion journey more worthwhile and effective, please do not hesitate to contact me. My contact information is at the end of this book. And always remember, we are in this together.

## Reflection questions to ponder:

- What are the obstacles to equity in your organization or community?
- What does your business say about the people you serve?
- What are the obstacles preventing you from learning from other cultures?
- What is your unconscious bias telling you about yourself?
- What can you and your organization do to harness diversity and support inclusive cultures?

# SUMMING IT UP

## DEI was never about race and gender only

It may have been introduced as such at first, but that was the first misunderstanding. DEI is about bringing diverse people with diverse lived experiences to co-create new ways of working and innovating together. This, in return, can increase the pie people need to share, so that more people have not just a stake in the business, but also a piece of pie. Now, all this pie talk is making me hungry. Furthermore, DEI does not mean hiring incompetent people. The problem is that someone might be turned down, not because they are incompetent, but solely based on their identity and background. This is where DEI policies are needed to right the wrong. Just like stock investments need a diversified portfolio to mitigate risk and increase performance, DEI is about hiring a diverse workforce to bring solutions to problems from diverse perspectives.

## DEI is not about homogenizing people

It is rather about diversity within diversity. Let me explain what I mean by that. Let's take a look at race, for example, because race in America is still a thorny topic. When you advance the rights of racial minorities, it's not about excluding other races. If, for instance, the inclusion of black people in leadership positions means excluding white people from those positions, then DEI has been done wrong. Inclusion is about including, not excluding. It should be about bringing more of the "others" to be a part of "us."

The fact is, even within a minority group, it's never homogeneous. *Why?* Because even within a single culture, there are various subcultures, social classes, and other differentials. Thus, DEI initiatives are about confronting discrimination, fighting inequalities within inequalities, and protecting minorities within minorities. And this includes all racial and ethnic backgrounds.

Addressing these problems at the local, national, and global levels is essential and requires both micro and macro approaches. Therefore, inclusion means looking at our differences but also acknowledging our commonalities — and celebrating them together. Thus, DEI is not about homogenizing people. It is about recognizing that there is diversity within diversity.

## Organizations should not be influenced by federal funding and abandon DEI initiatives.

If, as an organization, you were a beneficiary of the federal government funding of your DEI initiatives, you may be feeling the loss of its elimination, and that's a normal feeling. When something good is taken away, it's natural to feel a sense of loss. However, to simply abandon DEI just because the federal funding is no longer there, that's a whole other discussion.

Assess why you began the program in the first place. What was your motive? It's okay if you were driven by profits; there is no shame in admitting that. Then assess what you did right and what you may have missed. Was the program important? Why was it important? Do you think it succeeded in its goals? If yes, what do you attribute its success to? If not, what do you attribute its failure to?

Politicians come and go, but values are what organizational leaders should focus on. Were you genuinely advocating for DEI, or merely following trends? What sets you apart from those who treated DEI as a marketing gimmick — just a hashtag because it was becoming popular?

## DEI should be a leadership strategy

DEI should be incorporated into the operational strategy of the organization, and not just when things are good or less controversial. In other words, DEI should be about workplace culture transformation. It is about evaluating how things have always been done in a system that was created in an era when not everyone was represented in the workplace. Identify your target audience and consider generating more revenue by welcoming innovative ideas.

## DEI should not be a check-the-box

DEI is not a quick fix. Its success should be prioritized over a timeline, with the change going for long-term benefits over short-term instant gratification. It fails if organizations are only doing it because of federal funding.

## DEI was never about consensus

In a perfect world, everyone would be on board, especially because DEI has been well researched and documented as having a positive impact on organizations' bottom line. Ultimately, it was never about reaching a consensus. Just like the civil rights movement did not wait for consensus, and the women's suffrage movement, which championed women's right to vote in the US, was not dependent on consensus either. All movements that challenge the status quo are at first thorns in some people's sides, especially those who are not impacted by the lack of equity and inclusion.

Now, this is not to say that DEI is perfect. Nothing is perfect in this life. The intention may have been good, but perhaps the execution wasn't. But we will not know until we let it become a normal business operation that builds more equity and inclusion —and like anything else, it takes time.

## Balance is key

Everything under the sun is give and take, and we shouldn't take more than we are willing to give because it creates an imbalance. Even in nature, there is a balance that sustains life. We take oxygen from the trees and give them our carbon dioxide. (Okay, science enthusiasts, I see you!).

Some organizations were impatient in the execution of DEI initiatives, as if they should be able to press a button and *bam!* Many DEI programs may have failed because the employees who were put in charge of the work were not the ones with executive power. They may have been pressured to show the goods instantly or else. Some said they were burned out trying to prove the program's worth to high-level executives and even employees in general.

## DEI is the work of shifting mindsets

Many people also felt disenfranchised by its very nature, and it created a lot of skepticism. I have met people at my speaking events who told me that some in their workplaces viewed DEI as *"reverse racism,"* which might have fueled the current administration to take it down. This perception that *DEI is about race only* is not an accurate definition of diversity, whether these people believe it or not.

Furthermore, politicians use fearmongering to divide people, and it is clear that we do not only need to work on improving DEI programs but also on mindsets, particularly our own. Mindsets have to expand to see beyond our identity politics and come to the center to encounter one another in our differences to truly build something beautiful. For that to happen, we should all be responsible for DEI's success, as well as its shortcomings, so we won't need to place the blame when it fails. We are each responsible for the growth and expansion of our consciousness, and no one can change our perspective on things unless we want to.

## DEI is about the story we tell ourselves and others

Everyone has a *diversity* story, and we should not discount anyone just because they don't look like or pray like us, or have the same social status, or political affiliation, or any other identity construct.

Anything that touches our human emotions is complicated, and DEI matters are no different. I don't even know if we're going to fully succeed in understanding it, because it depends on where we are on our journey of self-actualization. But what I do know is that if we get together and help each other grow, first as a person and then as workers, we can achieve more than we could have expected.

The last thing I would caution organizational leaders is to be real and not overpromise, but expect surprises instead. And when these surprises arise, adjust accordingly. DEI is imperfect work done by imperfect humans who live imperfect lives in an imperfect world. Always remember *why*. Ultimately, in a so-called free enterprise, DEI should not be subject to executive orders. It should be an integral part of how businesses operate, reflecting a humanity-centered approach.

In finishing this book, let me congratulate you on your commitment to creating inclusive cultures, whether it is in your workplace or in the community where you live, work, and play. I am glad you chose my work as a tool to help you reflect and heal your own heart, so you can help heal your family, your community, your country, and your world.

Reflecting upon and giving a voice to life's moments can be empowering and even save lives. Many people think that suppressing hurt emotions or ignoring social issues can help them or society move on, but that only reinforces the trauma, both individual and collective trauma. Often, those suppressed emotions and issues resurface in a way that can be more destructive to ourselves and others. Cherish all moments, learn from each situation, and use them to empower yourself and others.

Unlocking the power of diversity provides an opportunity to overcome your own unconscious biases, connect with those who are different, and advocate for building inclusive cultures in the diverse and multicultural world we live in. Then you can create a ripple effect for social and economic justice—and lead from the heart and not the fear.

As you continue to discover and walk your path in life, you will find that even when things are going well, you may face challenges. As I said earlier, life is a cosmic dance, sometimes filled with paradoxical moments. It is a constant balancing act of good and bad, right and wrong, and everything in between. In these changing times, we need to evolve our mindsets. Your journey to becoming a conscious leader may take time but enjoy it as you move along the consciousness stages. Thank you for helping make the world a better place for all.

# GLOSSARY OF INCLUSIVE LEADERSHIP TERMS

Throughout this book, I used many diversity terms, and while this list is not exhaustive, it provides some diversity terms to help you become familiar with some of the language used in the diversity and inclusion field. As things evolve and future generations live in different realities, some of these terms may also change to fit the specific times and use.

## Belonging

Belonging can be defined as the feeling one has when they are accepted and valued within a social or work environment. When we feel a sense of belonging, we feel included and psychologically safe to share our knowledge to innovate or participate in activities that enhance the whole group.

## Bias

Bias can be conscious or unconscious. Conscious bias is an intentional choice to have prejudice, either favorably or unfavorably, toward a particular person or group because of who they are. An example of unfavorable conscious bias shows in the gender pay gap, where an employer might think women are not as smart or as hard-working as men, so the employer intentionally pays women a lower salary than men with the same qualifications and doing the same job.

Unconscious bias (also called implicit bias), on the other hand, is a perception that forms outside of our consciousness, but is also based on social stereotypes and often causes us to express prejudice in favor of or against someone or some groups based on their identity. Implicit biases are shaped by our lived experiences, as well as what we have been taught on how to make associations between specific qualities and social categories, including how we perceive racial differences, gender roles, and cultural norms. We need to bear in mind that not all unconscious bias is negative, and some might be needed to prevent unwelcome situations.

Most diversity training focuses only on unconscious bias because we all have it, and because conscious bias is a choice one makes intentionally, and no one else can change you unless you consciously choose to change. That is why unconscious bias training is needed to put it in the right context and do so without prejudice.

## Cross-Cultural Communication

Cross-cultural communication deals with how you communicate to enhance your cultural connections and effectively interact with others. There are similarities and differences in how people from different cultures communicate, whether verbally or non-verbally. There is a give and take. While you can learn something new about a different culture, you can also share something about your own culture. Even among people of the same culture, slight differences exist in how they communicate; there are subcultures within a larger ethnic group. For instance, even though they are all Asians, the Chinese, Japanese, Koreans, Vietnamese, and Indians all communicate differently.

## Color-Blind

The idea is that to get past racism, one only sees the person and not their race or the color of their skin. Although most people want to avoid racist behaviors, unfortunately, this thinking fails to see the real person for who they are or acknowledge their lived experiences, so it can be as offensive as being racist when someone says, "I don't see race or skin color," especially during diversity discussions.

## Colorism

Colorism, often found in Black communities and communities of color, is an issue stemming from internalized colonialism and racism that favors light-skinned individuals over those with darker skin. This issue has led to biased attitudes and discrimination based on a Black person's specific skin tone or shade, and it remains prevalent among Black individuals in Africa, the United States, and throughout the global Black diaspora.

## Cultural Diversity

Cultural diversity is the combination of the different ways people behave, work, live, learn, and express diverse perspectives, rooted in their cultural upbringing and life experiences.

## Cultural Fluency

Also termed as *cultural competency*, cultural fluency means the ability to engage in cultural settings different from our own. The term *fluency* is often interchanged with *competency or competence*, which is the overall goal of learning cultural diversity, and it implies both the ability and agility to work within and across cultures and to unlearn stereotypical and biased views based on differences between people (e.g., race or nationality), geographical locations (e.g., urban versus rural), generations (e.g., baby boomers versus millennials), and other diversity backgrounds and beliefs. Cultural fluency also assumes cultural sensitivity and humility.

## Cultural Humility

Cultural humility acknowledges our lack of understanding when it comes to otherness. It implies remaining humble and aware that none of us knows everything there is to know about ourselves, much less about others, specifically as it relates to cultural settings. It requires us to be reflective of our own cultural biases and stay on the learning journey about ourselves and others. An example we can often miss as Americans is the difference between being overly outspoken when sharing opinions.

Some people are okay with being reserved; however, this may be interpreted as being shy and, therefore, not confident. Or someone might prefer being independent versus interdependent because of the cultural values by which they were raised, and they will be okay with that. We have to stop imposing our cultural values on others and meet them where they are. Another example is having conservative versus liberal ideas. This has nothing to do with political parties. You can vote Democrat and still have some conservative beliefs, and vice versa. The point is not adhering to extremes when it comes to beliefs because with extremes comes extremism, fanaticism, and other negative *isms*. As long as you are an inclusive leader who believes in the power of diversity, equity, and inclusion, how you vote should be no one's business.

## Cultural Sensitivity

Cultural sensitivity reveals how well you understand and can engage with people whose cultural backgrounds are not the same as yours. You can raise your cultural sensitivity by taking training that helps you reduce cases of racial and other social prejudice based on negative stereotypes.

Learning all these cultural terms allows people to become more aware that there are differences in how people live, learn, and lead, and not to assume any one culture is better than others.

## Diversity

The best way to define diversity is to look at people's identity constructs, both seen and unseen. Diversity has many categories, including race, gender, ethnicity, national origin, ability (physical and mental), age, religious or spiritual practices, socioeconomic class or status, marital status, sexual orientation, political affiliation, veteran status, education, geographical location (for instance, urban versus rural), and work experience. Many people's diverse backgrounds can be easily perceived because of their physical appearances; however, more often than not, people also have some intrinsic traits that cannot be seen by the naked eye. These include, for example, the diversity of thoughts or diverse points of view on some issues, and the diversity of lived experiences. That is why it is paramount that all of us support and protect diversity. We must value each individual for who they are and what they contribute to the conversation to solve the world's diverse challenges and make it a better place for all.

## Equity

The quality of being fair and treating all people justly.

## Ethnic Groups

A group of people who identify with one another based on shared cultural practices. Some communities might also have differences within their cultures, so we have to acknowledge the subcultures.

## Inclusive Culture

An environment where everyone feels comfortable and accepted for who they are and encouraged to contribute their best work.

## Multicultural(ism)

This two-word term (**multi and cultural**) describes a society where more than one culture lives together. The United States is a multicultural society where many people from various countries and cultures live together. Achieving synergy among diverse cultures requires a strong commitment to respect each culture and recognize its invaluable contributions that enrich our society.

## People of Color

Currently, this term is the most used to include any US citizen who does not identify as only white or Caucasian under the current US Census ethnicity categories. Some people have expressed concern that this word might be considered racist, but I think they confuse it with the old term "colored people," which was used to refer to black people during segregation in America and was later considered derogatory.

## Privilege

The word privilege has several definitions depending on the context, but the one most pertinent to the reflections I shared in this book is where privilege means an advantage that is afforded to some people because of their race, culture, gender, religion, sexual orientation, ability or disability, and/or socioeconomic status. There is also an intersectionality in our different privileges. Some privileges may come from the circumstances one is born into, for example, being born into a royal family, while other privileges are from the rights one enjoys from living in a certain country or culture. For example, the right to basic education that every child in America has.

The term *white privilege,* however, can be difficult to accept for some white people because it is often associated with affluence. We know that not all white people are rich. But white privilege in the context of being white is when you don't face the same hurdles because of your white race, as people of other races do.

## Psychological Safety

Psychological safety refers to the feeling of safety, different from physical safety. When referring to the workplace, it is important for team building and performance. It fosters trust, facilitates learning, and helps resolve problems without fear of shame or punishment for mistakes. When there is psychological safety, you are encouraged to learn. This environment encourages open communication, collaboration, and innovation, as people are less likely to withhold information or feedback, and it fosters trust.

Of course, psychological safety is not a one-size-fits-all concept. You have to know your team well, both individually and collectively, as people can perceive it according to their individual culture and personal growth. But psychological safety is a key ingredient in any type of relationship. It refers to how people perceive the rewards or the consequences of taking interpersonal risks in a particular context, such as the workplace, in romantic relationships, or in group settings.

# NOTES

1. Choudhury, A., & Bainbridge, A. (2025, February 12). McKinsey Champions Diversity While Rivals Abandon Targets. *The Detroit News*. https://www.detroitnews.com/story/business/2025/02/12/mckinsey-champions-diversity-while-rivals-abandon-targets/78456726007/

2. Water Is Life. (2013). *First World Problems Read by Third World People*. https://youtu.be/LDLqafWub_o

3. Maslow, A. (1943). A Theory of Human Motivation. *Psychological Review*

4. Nimenya, S. (2016). We Are Not All That Different: Race and Cultural Identity. Organized by TEDx Sno-Isle Libraries. https://youtu.be/8QuAok_Xiyg

5. Lipman, V. (2017, April 15). *66% of Employees Would Quit If They Feel Unappreciated*. https://www.forbes.com/sites/victorlipman/2017/04/15/66-of-employees-would-quit-if-they-feel-unappreciated/

6. Cox, J. (2024, February 5). Stark Gender Gap Persists Among Young People's Attitudes toward Feminism, a survey shows. *Forbes*. https://www.forbes.com/sites/josiecox/2024/02/05/stark-gender-gap-persists-among-young-peoples-attitudes-toward-feminism-survey-shows/

7. Dina, K. (2018, September 25). New Zealand Prime Minister's Baby Makes History At U.N. General Assembly. The Guardian. Retrieved from https://www.npr.org/2018/09/25/651372487/new-zealand-prime-ministers-baby-makes-history-at-u-n-general-assembly

8. Beike Biotechnology. (2024). The Value of the Stay-at-Home Parent in 2024. https://beikecelltherapy.com/studies/the-value-of-the-stay-at-home-parent-in-2024.html

9. Bureau of Labor Statistics. (2025, April 23). https://www.bls.gov/news.release/pdf/famee.pdf

10. Barroso, A. (2021, January 25). For American couples, gender gaps in sharing household responsibilities persist amid the pandemic. Pew Research

Center. https://www.pewresearch.org/short-reads/2021/01/25/for-american-couples-gender-gaps-in-sharing-household-responsibilities-persist-amid-pandemic/

11. United Nations. Data on World Migration. Retrieved from https://www.un.org/en/development/desa/population/migration/data/index.asp

12. Newsday. (2019). Long Island Divided. https://projects.newsday.com/long-island/real-estate-agents-investigation/

13. Hunt, D. V., Layton, D., & Prince, S. (2015, January 1). Diversity matters. *McKinsey & Company*. Retrieved from: https://www.mckinsey.com/business-functions/organization/our-insights/why-diversity-matters

14. Arao, B., & Clemens, K. (2013). From Safe Spaces to Brave Spaces. In *The Art of Effective Facilitation: Reflections from Social Justice Educators*. ACPA Books, co-published with Stylus Publishing

15. World Bank. (2017). Migration and Remittances Data. https://www.worldbank.org/en/topic/migrationremittancesdiasporaissues/brief/migration-remittances-data

16. Budiman, A., & Connor, P. (2019, April 3). Remittances to the Sub-Saharan Africa Region. *Pew Research Center*. Retrieved from: https://www.pewresearch.org/fact-tank/2019/04/03/immigrants-sent-a-record-amount-of-money-home-to-sub-saharan-african-countries-in-2017/

# ABOUT THE AUTHOR

Seconde Nimenya is the author of five books and the founder and principal of BEChange Group˚ — a leadership and personal growth coaching firm. Seconde Nimenya is a speaker and inclusive leadership coach who has spent more than a decade as a thought leader on matters of diversity, equity, inclusion, and belonging, as well as personal development. She speaks at various conferences and in organizations in the United States and globally, inspiring her audiences to use their life experiences to better themselves and others.

Seconde works with business owners and organizational leaders who want to build inclusive workplaces and communities where everyone feels accepted for who they are and what they bring to the world to make it a better place for all. With more than ten years of experience as a professional in the field of global leadership and empowerment, she provides specialized work in the areas of building resilience and evolving through adversity.

Seconde Nimenya immigrated to North America in the 1990s, starting in Canada, where she lived for more than ten years before moving to the United States. In the US, she furthered her academic education and earned a master's degree in business administration, and she also holds a Graduate Certificate in Equity, Diversity, Inclusion, and Belonging Leadership from Harvard University. She blends her varied educational and cultural backgrounds to create insightful content and dynamic presentations, using a unique approach that is both inspiring and empowering.

Seconde Nimenya's TEDx talk on race and other identity constructs titled, *"We Are Not All That Different,"* has been hailed by many viewers as the most inspirational talk of our time. She has received community awards for her contributions to the work on personal growth and leadership development, recognizing her work in bridging the gaps between diverse and multicultural communities.

# BECHANGE GROUP COACHING AND TRAINING

**B**EChange Group® is a leadership coaching and personal growth firm founded by Seconde Nimenya. As the firm's principal coach and trainer, she offers the best in inclusive personal and professional leadership programs geared toward executives, people managers, diversity champions, and individuals who want to advance their understanding of diversity, equity, inclusion, and belonging.

At BEChange Group, we believe that by building a diverse workforce, your business will gain a competitive edge, your employees will thrive, and you will be able to build a legacy that will live on for centuries after you are gone.

This can only happen if, as an organizational leader, you are culturally fluent and can go beyond groupthink and increase problem-solving by harnessing the power of diversity, equity, and inclusion.

BEChange Group's clients range from global organizations, educational institutions, non-profit organizations, and businesses that need support in expanding their global reach, increasing their market share, and tapping into the possibilities offered by an ever-changing world. The team at BEChange Group is dedicated to your success. Check out our program offerings and contact us at: **www.BEChangegroup.com**.

# INVITE SECONDE NIMENYA
# TO SPEAK AT YOUR NEXT EVENT

Seconde shares thought-provoking, inspirational, and empowering insights with her audiences around the world. She is renowned for creating and facilitating meaningful presentations that change how teams interact, getting them to think in new and creative ways.

Her inspiring topics work well as keynotes, seminars, and workshops, and she supports organizations in exploring cultural enrichment—enabling them to engage effectively with individuals from diverse backgrounds in both professional and personal contexts.

To invite Seconde Nimenya to speak at your events, submit a request via the contact page on **www.BEChangegroup.com**.

# ALSO BY SECONDE NIMENYA

*Evolving Through Adversity:*
How do you discover who you are and use adversity to evolve and achieve your life's purpose? In this award-winning memoir, Seconde Nimenya answers the above question and demonstrates that the best way to get through adversity is to grow through it and learn from it. In this personal soul-searching book, Seconde recounts her life growing up in East Africa and her journey immigrating to North America, including fighting to obtain an education, learning hard lessons, and becoming a voice for others.

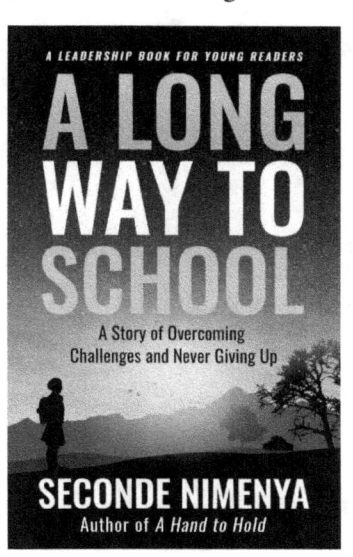

*A Long Way to School* is the adaptation of *Evolving Through Adversity,* retold for a young adult and teen audience, to inspire and empower them to overcome challenges in their school and personal lives.

Seconde invites young readers to deeply reflect on their own stories, and she shares leadership insights for the teen years and beyond to inspire young people on how to grow both personally and professionally.

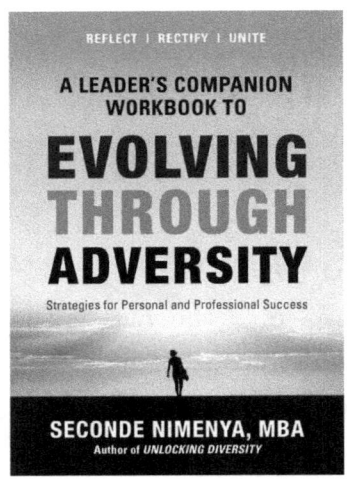

*A Leader's Companion Workbook to Evolving Through Adversity* is a step-by-step guide to personal and professional leadership development.

It provides a tangible and clear path for people to transform into their most authentic selves.

*A Hand To Hold* is Seconde Nimenya's debut novel about an Ethiopian orphan named Adina, who was adopted and brought to the United States at five years old.

This is a story of loss, love, redemption, and triumph over adversity—proving that life is a little easier when we have a hand to hold.

These books are available in paperback, eBook, and audiobook formats and can be found wherever books are sold.

www.ingramcontent.com/pod-product-compliance
Lightning Source LLC
Chambersburg PA
CBHW051645230426
43669CB00013B/2441